Bu:

& Bourbon

BURGOO, BARBECUE & BOURBON

A KENTUCKY CULINARY TRINITY

Albert W. A. Schmid

Photos by Jessica Ebelhar

Foreword by Loreal "Butcher Babe" Gavin

UNIVERSITY PRESS OF KENTUCKY

Paperback edition 2021
Copyright © 2017 by The University Press of Kentucky

Scholarly publisher for the Commonwealth,
serving Bellarmine University, Berea College, Centre College of Kentucky,
Eastern Kentucky University, The Filson Historical Society, Georgetown
College, Kentucky Historical Society, Kentucky State University, Morehead
State University, Murray State University, Northern Kentucky University,
Spalding University, Transylvania University, University of Kentucky,
University of Louisville, and Western Kentucky University.
All rights reserved.

Editorial and Sales Offices: The University Press of Kentucky
663 South Limestone Street, Lexington, Kentucky 40508-4008
www.kentuckypress.com

Library of Congress Cataloging-in-Publication Data

Names: Schmid, Albert W. A., author.
Title: Burgoo, barbecue, and bourbon : a Kentucky culinary trinity / Albert
    W. A. Schmid ; photos by Jessica Ebelhar ; foreword by Loreal "Butcher
    Babe" Gavin.
Description: Lexington, Kentucky : University Press of Kentucky, [2017] |
    Includes bibliographical references and index.
Identifiers: LCCN 2017010804| ISBN 9780813169880 (hardcover : alk.
paper) |
    ISBN 9780813169903 (pdf) | ISBN 9780813169897 (epub)
Subjects: LCSH: Barbecuing. | Cooking—Kentucky. | LCGFT: Cookbooks.
Classification: LCC TX840.B3 S278 2017 | DDC 641.7/6—dc23
LC record available at https://lccn.loc.gov/2017010804

ISBN 978-0-8131-5406-0 (pbk. : alk. paper)

This book is printed on acid-free paper meeting
the requirements of the American National Standard
for Permanence in Paper for Printed Library Materials.

Manufactured in the United States of America.

 Member of the Association
of University Presses

This book is dedicated to
my Kentucky parents, Richard E. and the late Carolyn S. Dunn.
Thank you for making me feel like your son.

Contents

Photographs follow page 90

Foreword

There's no place like home.

I cringe at the number of times I've packed up my life and hit the road. In the midst of chasing my dreams I often had no home. Within a decade of travel I had evolved from thrill-seeking dreamer, to a culinary student, to a suitcase, to a hotel room number, to a TV personality. Red lipstick and white knuckles quickly became part of my signature look. Bourbon is the mash of my signature flavor. Under the blazing lights and rolling cameras I found myself, and thus the "Butcher Babe" was born. I'd like to attribute my uncanny success to never forgetting where I came from and to the beautiful souls with whom I shared a stiff drink along the way.

I can honestly attest that I'd never felt at home on this green earth until I sprouted roots in the bluegrass of Louisville, Kentucky. It took me a few months to master the pronunciation of *Louisville* in its true Kentucky drawl, and once I did I also thoroughly enjoyed teaching others the "ways" of this remarkable place. From a culinary perspective, the cuisine here is hard to beat. Always has been, always will be. I love the way the people smile with their eyes and cook with their hearts. I have sensed a new ingredient, tastefully muddled among iconic flavors, that was at first hard to put my finger on. That timeless flavor I'm referring to is *love*. Bourbon also has a similar flavor profile, or at least that's what Albert taught me back in his Beer, Wine, and Spirits class at Sullivan University. It's impossible to deny the lasting impression a passionate man in a bow tie can have. Like an aged spicy rye, memories like this warm my bones and continue to fuel the flavors of my career. I'm not alone in this phenomenon. I am beyond elated to be a part of this timeless culture. If you aren't already familiar with this multifaceted man whom I affectionately call "chef," I feel it necessary to paint a picture for you. Albert is essentially the "Alton Brown" of the alcoholic beverage world. His list of accolades goes on longer than your great grandma's burgoo recipe. There's nothing squirrely about that.

It's simply nuts to assume that you can't find a little Kentucky in your heart. I have a piece of Kentucky with me everywhere I go. In fact, I happen to have a Maker's Mark bottle tattoo. I was a die-hard bourbon fan after I had my very first Old Fashioned. Iconic notes of citrus danced from my bourbon-baptized tongue right into my heart. Nearly a decade later, in the afternoon shade of an orange tree, my phone rang and for a moment broke my "California Dreamin'" state of mind. It was Albert. I have always loved catching up with him over the years, and on this particular day I could tell he was really jazzed about something. For a moment, I secretly imagined his bow tie was spinning with excitement. Please do that now. Thank you. You're welcome.

He asked me if I would write this foreword for him. As I gushed with honor, the fattest squirrel I've ever seen scampered out from the orange tree he'd been snacking on. Naturally, I fed him some of the granola I'd been snacking on and snapped some quick pictures with my new fur-friend. Albert and I both continued laughing, and he attested that this "squirrel omen" must be a sign, considering that burgoo isn't burgoo without squirrel meat in it. I asked if I should skin and dress the squirrel right there on the spot and wondered if he might taste like oranges. At that point in the conversation, Albert politely declined my dinner offering.

Cheers,
Loreal "Butcher Babe" Gavin

Preface

In 2011, Professor Jonathan Jeffrey, Manuscripts/Folklife Archives Coordinator of the Western Kentucky University's (WKU) library, invited me to Bowling Green to review a recent acquisition of more than 2,400 local and regional cookbooks that were a gift to the WKU special collections library. When I arrived, I found many of the volumes were wrapped in plastic to protect the books. So to access the information I had to remove the wrapping. Each time I would crack the plastic I had an excited feeling, as if I were opening a Christmas gift. Most of the volumes did not disappoint. The books were full of recipes, information from present day and from the past 150 years. Some of the books dated back to the late 1800s, most of them from the mid-1900s, but all of them were in some way related to Kentucky. In my opinion, this collection is a cultural treasure that chronicles Kentucky's gastronomic history. I was reminded of my graduate work in gastronomy at the University of Adelaide, where I studied the works of anthropologists Dame Mary Douglas and Claude Lévi-Strauss. Could this collection help reveal a change in Kentucky's cuisine? Would I find long-lost recipes? Or at the very least find common threads? In short, the answer to each of these questions was yes. The collection at WKU was so large that I had to make several trips to Bowling Green but only made a small dent in researching the collection. Some of my greatest discoveries were the handwritten notes: the stars next to great recipes, the substitutions of ingredients, or the addition of recipes not originally included by the author—either handwritten or clipped from a local paper. My ambition was always greater than the time I had with the collection. Many of the books I pulled off the shelves had to be returned at the end of the day without my ever having removed the plastic shield. None of the books could be checked out because they were part of the special collection—they had to stay at the library. I always left Bowling Green feeling I did not have enough time with the books. Kentucky State budget cutbacks, my teaching schedule, and the distance from Bowling Green would further complicate my access to this collection as the WKU library would close on Saturday and I could not take off teaching during the week. Fortunately, at the time, I worked at Sullivan University's National Center for Hospitality Studies. The NCHS has a national reputation for hospitality management, including the culinary arts and baking and pastry arts—so I knew that I had the resources to continue the research for this book.

During the past two decades I have witnessed a change as our supply chain has shifted, with the result that students' base knowledge of ingredients and of local and regional cuisines is narrower now as they enter into studying for their degrees. If any group has a vested interest in preserving and maintaining local and regional cuisines while looking to the future of cuisine, it would be culinary programs, their students and graduates. So I applied for and received a faculty grant through Sullivan University. The grant helped to defray the costs of some of my trips to Bowling Green but also allowed me to begin a collection of regional cookbooks when I hit the roadblock of state budget cuts and had to time trips to the library. In addition, the library staff at Sullivan University was very helpful in locating and borrowing books through the interlibrary loan program and the resources at the Sullivan University library.

Through the research of these many books I was able to find a change or evolution in several dishes and to rediscover several dishes that had been "lost" in Kentucky cuisine. Also the circumstances and events surrounding the consumption of Kentucky cuisine have changed, which is another reason why the cuisine has evolved over the past one hundred years. Kentuckians are very proud of the food and the hospitality that they provide their guests. This book explores some of the main pillars of Kentucky cuisine—I start with one of the most basic, burgoo, and build around this important dish, expanding burgoo to a complete meal that includes barbecue, side dishes, bread, beverages, and desserts. This is a cookbook to help preserve Kentucky cuisine.

Cheers,
Albert W. A. Schmid
Greensboro, North Carolina

1

Burgoo

Every area or region in the world has its own soup or stew, because soup and stew are nutritious, easy to fix, and economical. Popular legend holds that Parisian tavern-keeper Monsieur Boulanger opened the first modern "restaurant" in 1765, setting up shop in Paris's first arrondissement and hanging a sign that read, "Boulanger débite des restaurants divins" ("Boulanger provides divine sustenance"), with an invitation below in Latin: "Venite ad me omnes qui stomacho laboratis et ego vos restauro" ("Come to me, those who are famished, and I will give you sustenance"). The word *restaurant* comes from the "restorative" bouillon that the original restaurant served, a dish made from sheep feet in a white sauce. Even though the facts of this story and of Monsieur Boulanger's existence have been challenged by Rebecca Spang in her book *The Invention of the Restaurant: Paris and Modern Gastronomic Culture*, the fact remains that the modern restaurant was founded to serve something akin to a soup or stew. Today, most restaurants offer a soup or a stew as a choice at the beginning of the customer's meal.[1]

In the United States, soups and stews go by many regional names: ragout, gumbo, bogs, hotpots, chili, kettles, goulash, and chowder, to name a few. Kentucky's and Illinois's citizens are proud to put forth burgoo from their pots. Ronni Lundy writes in her book *Shuck Beans, Stack Cakes, and Honest Fried Chicken: The Heart and Soul of Southern Country Kitchens*, "If Gumbo is the national stew of Cajun country, burgoo is the stew of Kentucky." The word *burgoo* has several possible origins. It may have described an oatmeal porridge that was served to English sailors in the mid-

1700s, or it may have come from the small town of Bergoo (*sic*), West Virginia, which is in Webster County. The word might also be a slur of "birdstew" or perhaps "bulger"; it could also be a mispronunciation of "barbecue," "ragout," or an amalgam of the lot. If the oatmeal story is true, burgoo continued as a military staple as it became a hearty stew for soldiers who could travel light and hunt and gather ingredients "from wild things in the woods" once they stopped moving for the day—so they did not have to move the supplies from one location to another. Later, burgoo became a community event, made from "meat from domestic beasts and barnyard fowls with vegetable from the garden," which was many times connected to political campaigns—many of the politicians were former military heroes. Local women would have a "peeling party" for all of the vegetables that would go into the burgoo. Later that day, local men would tend to the burgoo pots all night while the mixture finished cooking.[2]

Burgoo is described in two ways, as a thin stew and/or as a thick soup that is cooked for a long time and is almost like a "chowder" in consistency. Vice president of the United States Alben Barkley of Paducah said, "A 'burgoo' is a cross between a soup and a stew, and into the big iron cooking kettles go, as we sometimes say in Kentucky, a 'numerosity' of things—meat, chicken, vegetables, and lots of seasoning." The *Mayfield Messenger*, the newspaper in Mayfield, Kentucky, said that "no one person probably will ever know how many different things are in a batch of burgoo" but that burgoo is "a six-course dinner all boiled in one . . . with the proper seasoning burgoo can't be anything but good and nutritious." However, no thickening agent is used in burgoo, and "no two burgoo recipes are exactly alike because this is a frontier dish." While some may look on burgoo as "just a glorified beef stew, just soupier," traditional burgoo includes squirrel in the recipe as well as a bird and some type of red meat. Burgoo originated as a wild game dish or a hunter's stew, as many recipes bear out, and is similar to Brunswick stew only more savory and spicy. However, it has been suggested that versions of burgoo containing "varmints" are palatable only with the bourbon chaser. A variety of vegetables are also used to make burgoo, including tomatoes, lima beans, onions, potatoes, okra, and corn. However, sweet vegetables are not used in burgoo. According to General James Tandy Ellis, cabbage should not be used to make burgoo even though many recipes include it. Wes Berry, author of *The Kentucky Barbecue Book* and professor at Western Kentucky University, writes that year-round availability of burgoo is limited to an area Berry has dubbed "the burgoo belt," which is in western Kentucky and runs from Daviess County in the north to Christian County in the south.[3]

There are competing claims on the invention of burgoo. One such claim comes from the Beard family of Kentucky. Another comes from a French chef, Gus Jaubert, who was known as the "burgoo King" and "the father of burgoo" in Lexington, Kentucky, and who became well known for his burgoo before or during the Civil War. According to legend, Chef Jaubert cooked for Confederate general John Hunt Morgan and his Raiders. Morgan's Raiders were known for marching "light and fast," which would have made living off the land very important. While Jaubert was in fact a Civil War veteran, the myth is busted by Robert Moss, author of *Barbecue: The History of an American Institution,* who points out that Jaubert served in the First Kentucky Infantry, not in Morgan's Second Kentucky Calvary. The Beard family's claim is strengthened by the fact that a twenty-one-year-old John Hunt Morgan was a member of Captain Oliver Hazard Perry Beard's company during the Mexican War. If General Morgan's regiment did make burgoo, could it be that General Morgan learned to make burgoo while serving under Cap-

tain Beard during the Mexican War? The Beard family's claim
is furthered by the fact that after his Civil War service, Jaubert,
according to Moss, "became involved with a Captain Beard and
Jake Hostetter, two veterans who had already established them-
selves before the war as respected Kentucky barbeque men." Years
later a baseball player named Oliver "Ollie" Perry Beard, the son
of Captain Beard, would continue the family tradition of making burgoo. In addition, Daniel "Uncle Dan" Beard, founder of
the Sons of Daniel Boone, a group that would eventually merge
with the Boy Scouts of America, wrote about burgoo in his book
Camp-Lore and Woodcraft. Uncle Dan wrote, "The burgoo and the
barbecue belong to that era when food was plenty, feasts were
generous and appetites good," and he continued with a recipe for
"the burgoo." Uncle Dan added, "All Kentuckians will vow they
understand the true meaning of the word 'burgoo.'" Jaubert may
have been the first person to marry burgoo and barbecue at the
same event, which happened to be a political rally for James B.
Beck, a Lexington lawyer running for Congress in 1866.[4] Eventually, Jaubert's crown would pass to J. T. Looney of Lexington.
Or it could be that burgoo is an evolved version of Brunswick
stew, which is very similar in composition, as is a stew from Wis-
consin and Minnesota called booyah (bouyah). In any case, the
secrets of burgoo may lie in the Lexington and Frankfort Cem-
eteries where Captain Beard, General Morgan, and the first burgoo king all rest.

Burgoo is an "outdoor, get-together" event most of the
time, taking many hours to prepare. Many of the early recipes
are huge—so large that they could literally feed an army. Burgoo also has political ties because in Kentucky, a political rally or
gathering that featured this dish was called a "burgoo." The two
burgoos (the political rally and the soup/stew) may have coincided
because burgoo (the soup/stew) is best "when fresh vegetables are

at their peak," mid- to late summer and early fall, and the political season is in full swing. Illinois's longest food festival is the Winchester Burgoo Festival, which originated in the late 1800s. Burgoo should be served with corn pones, cornbread, biscuits, or soda bread, and mint juleps, beer, or iced tea, with peach cobbler and vanilla ice cream or pie for dessert.[5]

Historic Burgoo Recipes

Some of these burgoo recipes are designed for a large group of people such as an army, a community get-together, or a political rally and are, therefore, not suggested to be made at home. However, these recipes are important because they help us understand how they were once used to bring a community together (and how much of that community is brought together) and how our society has changed over the years (requiring smaller recipes). There are recipes toward the end of this chapter that are more appropriate for home use.

The first recipe for burgoo (Kentucky burgout [*sic*]) is adapted from *The Blue Grass Cookbook*, a 1904 classic by Minnie C. Fox.[6] This recipe includes several items that identify it as a burgoo, such as the squirrels, birds, tomatoes, and corn, and does not contain cabbage. However, this recipe also has a few items found in very few burgoos: the barley and the oysters.

Kentucky Burgout (*sic*)

12–15 servings

6 squirrels
6 birds
1½ gallons water

1 tea cup pearl barley
1 quart tomatoes
1 quart corn
1 quart oysters
1 pint sweet cream
¼ pound butter
2 tablespoons flour
seasonings

Boil the squirrels and birds in the water until tender, and remove all the bones. Add the barley and vegetables and cook slowly for 1 hour. Ten minutes before serving, add the oysters and cream with butter and flour rubbed together. Season to taste and serve hot.

Please note: "Flour and butter rubbed or kneaded together," like a beurre manié, is used for sauces and soups to thicken, as one would use a roux. The difference (and this is important) is that a roux is usually used hot with a cold stock, while a beurre manié is used cold with a hot stock or soup. To use a hot roux with a hot stock or a cold with cold would allow the flour to clump, which means the resulting sauce would be lumpy. The beurre manié is used to finish the sauce or soup. The chef can add as needed.

This second recipe for burgoo is, perhaps, the best representation of a basic burgoo that calls for living off the land and using what you have available. However, this recipe is based on a relatively recent source. The inclusion of game meat suggests that this is an old recipe, something that early soldiers might pull together, but it comes from *The Monterey Cookbook*, which was published in 1986 and refers to the town of Monterey in Owen County; both the town and the county have military ties.[7] The town of Monterey is named for the Battle of Monterey, which was fought during the Mexican-American War and would make the American commanding officer Major General Zachary "Old Rough and Ready" Taylor a national hero. Taylor eventually became the twelfth president of the United States but would serve less than a year and a half before dying of a stomach ailment. President Taylor is buried in Louisville, Kentucky, at the Zachary Taylor National Cemetery. The cemetery sits on land that was part of a land grant to Taylor's father, Colonel Richard Taylor, for his Revolutionary War service, and now has more than fourteen thousand interments. Owen County is named for Colonel Abraham Owen, who served as an aide-de-camp to Major General William Henry Harrison, the future ninth president of the United States, at the Battle of Tippecanoe, where Colonel Owen was killed in 1811 while US forces battled Native American warriors led by Shawnee leader Tecumseh.

This is a large recipe yielding fifty gallons, but it is important to show both the game in the burgoo and the large batching, both of which are traditional to burgoo.

Monterey Burgoo

50 gallons

40 pounds beef
25–30 pounds deer meat
10 squirrels
5 wild rabbits
6–8 chickens
2 groundhogs
5 pounds beef suet
25 pounds potatoes
20 pounds onions
10 pounds carrots

100 ears field corn, shucked and corn cut from the ear
1 bushel tomatoes
3 or 4 heads cabbage
10 pounds green beans
18–20 quarts tomato juice
6 ounces black pepper
1½ ounces red pepper
6 jalapeno peppers, chopped
6 cayenne peppers, chopped
1 pound salt

In a very large kettle, cover all the meat and beef suet with water and cook for 4 hours. Remove bones from meat. Bring back to a boil and add the hard vegetables (potatoes, onions, carrots, and corn). Let them boil for 2 hours. Let the fire die down and add remaining vegetables. Add tomato juice. Add salt and pepper, red pepper, jalapeno peppers, and cayenne peppers. Let simmer very slowly for 1 hour. You can almost let the fire go out because the kettle will retain enough heat to simmer the burgoo. Stir constantly (or as often as possible) the entire time.

Illinois is also known for burgoo. Franklin, Illinois, is known as the "Burgoo Capital of the World," but then so are Lawrenceburg and Owensboro, Kentucky. The village of Franklin is located in Morgan County, which is named for Major General Daniel Morgan, a cousin of Daniel Boone, who served in the Revolutionary War—he was the victorious commander at the Battle of Cowpens—and during the Whiskey Rebellion. General Morgan's Riflemen were known for their guerrilla tactics; many times they targeted British officers first. Ironically, John Hunt Morgan claimed to be a descendant of General Morgan.

This recipe is recast from *Brighton, Illinois, Centennial Cookbook*—"to provide nutritious, satisfying, and delectable meals for the next one hundred years." Please note the addition of navy beans, which are not usually found in Kentucky burgoo, although Dan Beard lists beans in his recipe.[8] Lima beans are usually found in Kentucky burgoo. Beard claims Kentucky as the origin of burgoo.

Brighton Burgoo Soup

400 gallons

200 pounds potatoes
200 pounds navy beans
8 bushels tomatoes (24 #10 cans)
16 bushels sweet corn (24 #10 cans)
200 pounds onions
60 fat hens
120 pounds beef brisket
60 pounds smoked pork jowl
400 pounds beef bones
water as needed

Combine all ingredients and cook (simmer) for about 24 hours. Season to taste.

Note: other vegetables may be added, if desired.

In 1931 the United States was in the midst of the Great Depression. Politicians were gearing up for the election of 1932. Franklin D. Roosevelt was about to become president, and Prohibition was about to be repealed. This early recipe is designed to serve thousands of people—which would have helped draw voters to a political event because so many people were out of work; by some estimates one out of every three people in Kentucky was unemployed just because of the bourbon industry—so the number was much higher. In a time before mass media, this was how political candidates were able to gather crowds to hear their messages; today, with radio and television and the Internet, rallies such as the one described here are of much lesser importance. For this event Dr. Bow Reynolds was the "master of affairs and chief cook," and the *Mayfield Messenger* newspaper reported his recipe to eager readers. Later, *True Tales of Old-Time Kentucky Politics: Bombast, Bourbon & Burgoo* revived the recipe, from which the following is adapted.[9]

Dr. Bow Reynolds Burgoo

10,000 servings (?)

1½ tons beef
½ ton pork
40 bushels potatoes
40 bushels onions
480 (16-ounce) cans tomatoes
40 bushels carrots
1,200 roasting ears corn
40 gallons peas
1 bushel red peppers
1 gallon garlic

Divide all ingredients among as many large kettles as necessary. Fill the kettles with water, and cook until meat is done.

The Southern Cook Book of Fine Old Recipes, compiled and edited by Lillie S. Lustig, S. Claire Sondheim, and Sarah Rensel, first appeared in 1935. In it, the authors present a huge recipe that yields 1,200 gallons. They claim that the recipe originated from a handwritten copy of J. T. Looney's Burgoo. Looney was recognized as the "Burgoo King," and E. R. Bradley named Kentucky Derby winner Burgoo King in honor of Looney.[10]

Burgoo for a Huge Crowd

1,200 gallons

600 pounds lean soup meat (no fat, no bones)
200 pounds fat hens
2,000 pounds potatoes, peeled and diced
200 pounds onions
5 bushels cabbage, chopped
60 (10-pound) cans tomatoes
24 (10-pound) cans puréed tomatoes
24 (10-pound) cans carrots
18 (10-pound) cans corn
red pepper and salt to taste
Worcestershire, Tabasco, or A-1 Sauce

Mix the ingredients, a little at a time, and cook outdoors in huge iron kettles over wood fires for 15–20 hours. Use squirrels in season: 1 dozen squirrels to each 100 gallons of burgoo. Season to taste.

General James Tandy Ellis (1869–1942) was many things in his life—a journalist, author, musician, and humorist—and during World War I he was the adjutant general of Kentucky for the National Guard. He was born in Ghent, Kentucky, in Carroll County (named for Charles Carroll, the oldest and the last surviving signer of the Declaration of Independence) to Dr. Peter Clarkson and Drusilla Tandy Ellis. He was married to Harriet Bainbridge Richardson. Ellis became a disciple of Gus Jaubert, learning how to make burgoo directly from the King himself. Marion Flexner, author of the Kentucky classic *Out of Kentucky Kitchens*, wrote that she published a recipe that Ellis objected to because it contained cabbage.[11] Ellis died on December 9, 1942, two days after his wife's birthday, at the age of seventy-four. Heartbroken, his wife, Harriette, died less than two months later, on January 24, 1943. The following is inspired by the recipe that Ellis sent to Flexner. The large variation in serving size suggests that the average serving was larger in the past, supporting Uncle Dan's observation.

Tandy Ellis's Burgoo

8–20 servings

2 pounds beef, cut from the shank (soup bone included)
½ pound lamb (baby lamb, not mutton)
1 medium chicken
2 cups diced potatoes
red pepper to taste (1 small pod, or more to taste)
3 cups corn cut from the cob (young field corn is best)
salt and black pepper to taste
1 "toe" (clove) garlic
2 cups onions, diced
2 cups fresh butter beans, or 1 package frozen butter beans
3 carrots, diced
1 cup parsley, minced
2 green peppers, diced, seeds removed

2 cups okra, diced or cut into rings
4 quarts water, or more if soup cooks too thick
12 tomatoes, or 1 quart can

Put the beef, lamb, and dismembered chicken in a soup kettle with water, salt, and black and red pepper. Ellis specified an old-fashioned iron kettle, but any heavy aluminum or metal kettle with a tight-fitting lid will do. Let the meat come to a hard boil, reduce the heat, and simmer about 2 hours with the lid on. Add potatoes and onions, and at intervals of 10 minutes, the butter beans, carrots, and green peppers. Then add corn and simmer for 2 hours or until the mixture seems very thick. Watch carefully so that it does not stick. Add more water from time to time if necessary, but use as little as possible. Add okra, tomatoes, and garlic and let simmer another 1½ hours, or until these vegetables too are done and blended with the others. The soup should cook for 4–7 hours. This soup improves by standing and can be kept for a long time in the refrigerator. Serve with corn pones; follow with a piece of pie.

In 1976 Nancy and Arthur Hawkins authored *The American Regional Cookbook: Recipes from Yesterday and Today for the Modern Cook*. They divide the cuisine of the United States into nine regions; Kentucky cuisine was classified as part of "Southern cooking." Burgoo is classified as a "meat," not as a "soup." The Hawkinses point out that "the burgoo is an outdoor get-together happening," and in their book they feature three recipes: a very old recipe, an old recipe, and a "more reasonable recipe" for burgoo.[12] It is interesting to note that the "very old recipe" contains oats, which would have been part of the original recipe for burgoo. The following are adapted from their book:

Very Old Recipe for Burgoo

100 pounds beef
12 chickens
1½ bushels potatoes
1 peck turnips
1 peck carrots
1 gallon onions
30 tomatoes
12 ears corn, cut from the cob
3 boxes oatmeal
4 pounds salt
¾ pound pepper
12 heads cabbage

Combine all ingredients in a large kettle or kettles, covering the contents with water. Cook/simmer for 24 hours.

Old Recipe for Burgoo

24–30 servings

6 squirrels
6 chickens
6 pounds beef
lots of tomatoes
lots of corn
lots of onion
lots of peppers
(The amounts and ratios of the vegetables are at the cook's discretion.)

Combine all ingredients in a large kettle, covering the contents with water. Cook/simmer for 24 hours.

Reasonable Recipe for Burgoo

8–10 servings

1 young squirrel, dressed and jointed
1 young chicken, dressed and jointed
1½ pounds beef, cut into 2-inch cubes
1½ pounds pork, cut into 2-inch cubes
several tomatoes, skinned and quartered
kernels cut from 6 ears corn
1 red pepper, cut up
5 green peppers, cut up
5 onions, peeled and quartered
2 teaspoons salt
1 teaspoon pepper
¼ teaspoon cayenne pepper

Cover the meat with water, using a heavy pot or kettle, and simmer slowly 4–5 hours or until meat is well done and most of the water is cooked away.

Add the vegetables and seasonings and whatever more water may be necessary.

Serve with hunks of soda bread and mint juleps or beer.

Note: "Jointed" means to cut at the joint. This does several things. It allows exposure of the cartilage (which is good for stock and soup) but also allows the meat to be removed easily.

Margaret M. Bridwell's book *Kentucky Fare: A Recipe Book of Some of Kentucky's Mouth Watering Specialties* is small but hits all of the classic Kentucky dishes. Written in 1953, it begins, "Kentuckians are proud of being famous for an inherent hospitality. . . ." Bridwell suggests that burgoo be served with "corn pones, a green salad and fruit pie" for a "completely satisfying meal."[13] This recipe is based on her burgoo.

Burgoo

15–20 servings

2 pounds lean beef, with bone
1 medium hen
1 pound veal
4 quarts water
6 ears young corn, cut from cob
2 cups rock potatoes, diced
2 cups onion, diced
1 pint fresh or frozen butter beans
3 carrots, diced
2 cups okra, diced
2 green peppers, diced
1 button garlic
1 small pod red pepper
1 cup parsley, minced
1 quart tomatoes
1 stalk celery, diced
bacon fat

In a heavy aluminum or iron kettle with a tight lid, boil the beef, veal, and chicken in the water until they are very tender. Remove meat and separate from bones. Replace meat in pot. Fry onions in bacon fat until yellow. Add to meat and stock. Add potatoes, carrots, and celery. Cook about 15 minutes. Add butter beans and cook about 2 hours, simmering slowly. The mixture should be very thick. If too thick, add a small amount of water from time to time to prevent sticking. Add okra, tomatoes, garlic, and red pepper pod. Let simmer another hour. Add corn and cook 30 minutes. Stir in parsley when ready to take from stove. Salt to taste.

This recipe is adapted from *Kentucky's Best: Fifty Years of Great Recipes* by Linda Allison-Lewis.[14] This burgoo is the most complex recipe featured and comes from the Honorable Order of Kentucky Colonels when they held an annual Derby barbecue. The Order discontinued the Derby Barbecue in 2008.

Kentucky Colonels' Burgoo

150 servings

8 pounds pork
1 pound veal
6 pounds breast of lamb
30 pounds beef
20 pounds chicken
20 pounds turtle meat
1½ gallons tomato purée
1 pound barley
1 gallon white corn, cut
1 gallon whole cranberries
1 gallon small mushrooms, chopped
1 gallon turnips, diced
3 pounds Irish potatoes, quartered
10 pounds onions, chopped
20 green peppers, quartered
1 gallon carrots, sliced
5 pounds cabbage, sliced

1 gallon okra, chopped
1 gallon celery, diced
3 tablespoons pepper
2 cups salt
6 ounces horseradish roots, finely grated
¼ cup Worcestershire sauce
3 tablespoons Italian-style seasoning
1 cup fresh parsley, chopped
1½ tablespoons bay leaves
10 pods red pepper, well pulverized
1½ tablespoons oregano
3 tablespoons chili seasoning

The day before the burgoo is to be served—start at noon—cook meat in huge kettles over an open fire, simmering overnight. The next day, divide meat and mix it together in 6 or 7 huge kettles. Add vegetables and seasonings and cook them with meat, simmering about 4 hours.

MORE RECENT BURGOO RECIPES

The burgoo recipes in this section are smaller and more manageable for the home cook who needs to feed fewer than twenty people. They also feature the creativity of the cooks who created these recipes and put their own stamp on a classic Kentucky dish.[15]

The *Louisville Courier-Journal & Times Cookbook* by Lillian Marshall, which included ninety-one favorite Cissy Gregg recipes, is a Kentucky cuisine classic. The book features two recipes for burgoo, one from Hart County and the other from Wayne County. Both counties are named for soldiers. Hart County is named for Captain Nathaniel Gary Smith Hart, son of Colonel Thomas Hart and his wife, Susanna Grey Hart. Captain Hart was a graduate of Princeton, a Lexington lawyer and businessman who volunteered during the War of 1812 with the Lexington Light Infantry. His company was captured at the Battle of Frenchtown (also known as the Battle of the River Raisin). Captain Hart died the next day, with many of his men, in the Massacre of River Raisin at the hands of the Native Americans who were allied with the British; he had been betrayed by a former Princeton classmate, William Elliott, who was a captain for the British Army. Hart County is one of nine counties in Kentucky named for officers who fought in the Battle of Frenchtown. The others include Allen County, Ballard County, Edmonson County, Graves County, Hickman County, McCracken County, Meade County, and Simpson County. Hart County burgoo is also featured in *Cabbage Patch: Famous Kentucky Recipes*; in *Favorite Fare II*, a cookbook by the Woman's Club of Louisville, as "Cissy Gregg's Kentucky Burgoo"; in *Kentucky Kitchens, Volume II* as burgoo; in *The Courier-Journal Kentucky Cookbook*, edited by John Finley, as "Kentucky Burgoo"; and in Tom Hoge's *The Bourbon Cookbook* with the addition of 6 ounces of bourbon. For many people this recipe, amalgamated from the sources just cited, could be viewed as the gold standard for burgoo. This burgoo also freezes well.[16]

Hart County Burgoo

12 quarts

2 pounds pork shank
2 pounds veal shank
2 pounds beef shank
2 pounds breast of lamb
4-pound hen
8 quarts water

1½ pounds potatoes, pared and diced
1½ pounds onions, peeled and diced
1 bunch carrots, diced
2 green peppers, diced
2 cups cabbage, chopped
1 quart tomato purée
2 cups whole corn, fresh or canned
2 pods red pepper
2 cups okra, diced
2 cups lima beans
1 cup celery, diced
salt and cayenne to taste
parsley, chopped
Tabasco to taste
A-1 sauce to taste
Worcestershire sauce to taste

Put all the meat and cold water in a 4-gallon kettle and bring slowly to a boil. Simmer until the meat is tender enough to fall from the bones. Lift the meat out of the stock; let cool, then chop the meat, removing the bones.

Return meat to stock and add potatoes and onions. Stir frequently with a long-handled spoon or paddle. Add remaining vegetables. Allow to simmer until thick, stirring almost constantly when stew thickens. Burgoo should be very thick but still "soupy." Season as it cooks, but not too much until almost done. Add parsley just before the stew is ready to serve.

Total cooking time is approximately 10 hours.

Wayne County is named for Major General Anthony "Mad Anthony" Wayne, who served with distinction during the Revolutionary War and after as the commander in chief of the Army of the United States. Wayne was also a member of the US House of Representatives, representing Georgia's First Congressional District during the Second Congress.[17] This recipe, named after Wayne County, also freezes well.

Wayne County Burgoo

12–15 servings (7 quarts)

2½ pounds meaty shank of beef
3 pounds chicken
bacon fat
salt to taste
½ quart canned or fresh tomatoes
1 cup celery, diced
2 cups potatoes, diced
2 cups carrots, diced
2 cups fresh corn, cut from the cob
1 cup green beans, cut
1 cup peas
1 package frozen lima beans
1 small can white soup beans
½ cup okra, sliced
1 teaspoon pepper
¼ teaspoon crushed red pepper (or more, to taste)
2 teaspoons sugar
1 can unseasoned chicken broth or water for thinning
½ cup flour, mixed with a cup of cream for thickening

The day before serving: Brown beef in bacon fat. Add cold water to cover and add chicken and salt. Simmer, loosely covered, until

meats are tender. Chicken will get done first; remove it and refrigerate, covered. Continue cooking the beef until very tender;
remove and refrigerate, covered. Strain broth and refrigerate.

The day of serving: Skim fat from broth; remove chicken
and beef from bones. Set aside. Measure the broth into a large
kettle, at least 8-quarts size, and add water to total 3 quarts. Add
vegetables and seasonings and simmer, loosely covered, for at least
2 hours, the slower and longer, the better. Stir often from the
bottom. If the stew seems to be getting too thick, add water or
chicken broth.

Preheat oven to 300 degrees F. Cut the meat in bite-size
pieces and place in an oven-going container. Toss well to mix the
meats and place in oven, covered, to heat for at least 1 hour. By
this time the soup should be very thick but still "soupy." If it seems
thin, add flour mixed with cream and cook, stirring until well
thickened. Season to taste.

To serve, place squares of egg cornbread in bottoms of large
soup bowls and ladle the soup onto the bread. Spoon the hot meat
on top of each serving.

In 1988 Kentucky native Charles Patteson wrote a book on Kentucky cuisine called *Charles Patteson's Kentucky Cooking.* Having
eaten burgoo all of his life, Patteson discusses the use of filé powder, which can be used to flavor and thicken the burgoo. He warns
not to use filé if you plan to reheat your burgoo because the filé
will become stringy and the burgoo will become gummy. Another recipe for burgoo from the book *Historic Homes—Kentucky
Heritage Recipes* includes filé in the recipe. The addition of filé is
not common to recipes of burgoo but is very common in gumbo. Patteson also uses curry powder, which was one of Burgoo
King T. J. Looney's many secret ingredients, in addition to An-

gostura bitters, Worcestershire sauce, tomato catsup, and sherry wine.[18] Taylor County is named for President Zachary Taylor, who is mentioned earlier in this chapter. The following is inspired by Patteson's burgoo.

Charles Patteson's Taylor County Burgoo

16–18 servings, as a first course

1 whole stewing chicken (4½–5 pounds)
4 cups beef stock or broth
6 large ripe tomatoes
2 medium onions, unpeeled
2 teaspoons curry powder
1 tablespoon black pepper, freshly ground
1 tablespoon coarse (kosher) salt
1½ cups bourbon
2 skinless, boneless chicken breasts, cut into two pieces
1 cup country ham trimmings, diced (optional)
2 cups fresh or frozen corn kernels, thawed if frozen
1 cup raw potatoes, diced
2 cups fresh lima beans, shelled
2½ cups okra, trimmed of stems and halved lengthwise
1 tablespoon filé powder (optional)

Place the chicken in a large stockpot with beef stock and enough water to cover. Bring to a boil over high heat. Reduce the heat to a simmer and skim off the foam as it rises to the surface. When the broth is clear, add the tomatoes, onions, curry powder, salt, and pepper. Cover partially and simmer gently for 2 hours.

Add 1 cup of the bourbon; partially cover and simmer for another 2 hours.

Turn off the heat. Remove the chicken. Trim off and discard the skin and bones. Reserve the meat in large pieces. Strain the soup into another container; press the onion in the tomato pulp through the sieve into the broth. Discard the solids. Chill until the fat can be readily skimmed from the surface.

Rinse the stockpot and return the soup to it. Add the remaining ½ cup bourbon, the reserved chicken meat, and the raw chicken breast meat. Add the ham, corn, potatoes, lima beans, and okra. Cover partially and simmer for 30 minutes. Season to taste.

Jeff Maxwell's book *Secrets of the M*A*S*H Mess: The Lost Recipes of Private Igor* highlights Maxwell's tenure as a recurring character on the hit TV series.[19] The show was based on the award-winning film *MASH*, which is based on the novel by Richard Hooker, *MASH: A Novel about Three Army Doctors*. A MASH unit was a Mobile Army Surgical Hospital, and these hospitals were operational from 1945 to 2006. They have since been replaced with Combat Support Hospitals (CSH—pronounced *cash*). Maxwell's book is filled with remembrances, photos, and recipes, which were highlighted in the TV series that ran for eleven seasons from 1972 to 1983 and won forty-four awards. The cast featured Alan Alda, Loretta Swit, Jamie Farr, Gary Burghoff, Wayne Rogers, William Christopher, McLean Stevenson, Larry Linville, Harry Morgan, David Ogden Stiers, and Maxwell as Private Igor, the bumbling cook of M*A*S*H 4077. Including burgoo in his cookbook, Maxwell ironically confirms the military roots of this stew and the fact that his was a mobile unit that might need to forage for ingredients—although there is no proof that Maxwell considered that when he included the recipe in his cookbook about the fictional army unit. Also, the idea that this stew was perhaps served at a military unit that was charged with restoring the health of soldiers goes to the restorative quality of soup and stew. The following recipe is adapted from Maxwell's:

The Battle of Burgoo

12 servings

4 pounds beef shanks
4 pounds chicken, cut into quarters
3 quarts chicken broth (or beef broth)
3 cups canned plum tomatoes (or 6 plum tomatoes, peeled, seeded, and chopped)
3 cups tomato purée
6 medium russet potatoes, quartered
6 carrots, peeled and thinly sliced
2 medium yellow onions, chopped
2 cups corn kernels
1½ cups cabbage, shredded
1 cup celery, sliced
1 cup okra, thinly sliced
3 tablespoons Worcestershire sauce
1 tablespoon Tabasco sauce
1 teaspoon black pepper
½ teaspoon salt
2 cups frozen peas
1 cup parsley, chopped

In a large heavy kettle combine the beef, chicken, and broth. Bring to a simmer and cook slowly until the meats are very tender and fall from the bones, about 2½ hours.

Remove the beef and chicken from the broth and chop into chucks. Discard the bones and return the meats to the broth.

Add all of the remaining ingredients except the peas and parsley. Simmer slowly, stirring occasionally, over low heat for about 2 hours or until the vegetables are soft and the stew is very thick.

Add the peas and parsley and cook for 10 minutes.

Serve with crusty bread and additional Tabasco sauce on the side.

❦

This next recipe is inspired by *Mountain Laurel Encore: A Collection of Recipes*, a cookbook published by the Bell County Extension Homemakers of Bell County, Kentucky, in 1984. The name of the recipe suggests that other burgoo is less delicious or, worse, the opposite of delicious. There are several ingredients not found in other burgoos—bacon fat and brown sugar—and this burgoo is thickened with butter and flour.

Bell County is named for statesman Joshua Fry Bell, the son of David and Martha Fry Bell. Bell was a graduate of Centre College and Transylvania Law School. He was elected to Congress in 1844 but served only one term (March 4, 1845—March 3, 1847). He later served as the secretary of state for Kentucky (July 2, 1849—March 16, 1850) and as a representative in the Kentucky House of Representatives (1862—1867). He was highly regarded, being nominated by the Union Democrats for governor of Kentucky, but he declined the nomination. Bell represented Kentucky at the Peace Conference of 1861 in Washington, DC, with the hopes of preventing the US Civil War. He died in Danville, Kentucky, in 1870.

Delicious Burgoo

10 servings

3 tablespoons bacon fat
1 pound beef stew meat
1 chicken, quartered
2 quarts water
2 teaspoons salt
1½ cups onions, chopped
1 clove garlic, minced
1 cup potatoes, diced
4 stalks celery, diced
1 can (1 pound, 3 ounces) tomatoes
3 carrots, diced
1 cup green pepper, chopped
8–10 ounces frozen lima beans
$^1/_8$ teaspoon crushed red pepper
1 bay leaf
2 teaspoons brown sugar
¼ teaspoon black pepper
1 cup okra, sliced
8 ounces frozen corn
¼ cup butter
½ cup flour
¼ cup parsley, chopped

In a large Dutch oven combine 2 tablespoons bacon fat and beef. Brown meat on all sides. Add chicken, water, and salt. Cover and cook slowly over medium heat until meat is tender. Remove beef and chicken. Remove chicken from bones and discard bones. Cut beef and chicken into large pieces. Return chicken and beef to broth. In a frying pan cook onions in remaining bacon fat until tender; add onions to broth. Add garlic, potatoes, celery, tomatoes, carrots, green pepper, beans, red pepper, bay leaf, brown sugar, and pepper. Cook slowly, stirring occasionally for 2 hours.

Add okra and corn and cook for 15 minutes. In a bowl, combine butter and flour; blend into burgoo. Sprinkle with parsley before serving.

MODERN BURGOOS

James Villas is a James Beard Award–winning author who wrote the book *Stews, Bogs & Burgoos: Recipes from the Great American Stewpot*, which includes recipes for three different burgoos, a traditional Kentucky burgoo, a Tennessee quail burgoo, and Veal, Corn, and Mushroom Burgoo. Villas writes that he discovered this last recipe while attending a dinner sponsored by Brown-Forman, the parent company of Jack Daniel's, at the Kentucky Derby. He indicates that veal breast might be difficult to work with but that it is "flavorful" and "there is really nothing like it."[20] The following recipe is based on his creation:

James Villas's Veal, Corn, and Mushroom Burgoo

4–6 servings

1 5-pound breast of veal, trimmed of excess fat and cut into
   2-inch pieces
2 tablespoons all-purpose flour
¼ cup (½ stick) butter
1 tablespoon vegetable oil
2 large onions, chopped
1 clove garlic, minced
1 cup chicken stock or broth
1 cup water
2 tablespoons tomato paste
2 large, ripe tomatoes, chopped and juices retained
½ teaspoon dried thyme, crumbled

salt and freshly ground black pepper to taste
12 medium-sized mushrooms, quartered
2 cups fresh or frozen corn kernels

Dredge the veal pieces in the flour, tapping off any excess. In a large, heavy pot, heat 2 tablespoons of the butter plus the oil over moderately high heat, then add the veal and brown on all sides. Tipping the pot, pour off all but about 1 tablespoon of the fat; then add the onions and garlic and stir for 1 minute. Add the stock, water, and tomato paste and stir till well blended. Add the tomatoes and their juices, thyme, salt, and pepper. Bring the liquid to a boil, reduce the heat to a gentle simmer, cover, and cook until the veal is tender, about 2¼ hours.

In a medium-size skillet, heat the remaining 2 tablespoons of butter over moderate heat, then add the mushrooms and stir until slightly browned, about 5 minutes. Add the mushrooms to the veal along with the corn, increase the heat to moderately high, and stir for 2–3 minutes before serving.

Sharon Thompson is a food writer for the *Lexington Herald-Leader* and author of the cookbook *Flavors of Kentucky.* Thompson writes, "Keeneland's burgoo recipe is virtually the same as it was in 1936, except for the type of meat used." The following dish is adapted from a recipe from Turf Catering, which ran the Keeneland concessions in 2006. [21]

Kentucky Burgoo

18–20 servings

oil
3 pounds stew meat

1 teaspoon ground thyme
1 teaspoon sage
1 teaspoon oregano
1 teaspoon garlic, minced
1 cup celery, diced
1 cup carrot, diced
1 cup onion, diced
12-ounce can diced tomatoes in juice
2 16-ounce cans mixed vegetables
7-ounce can tomato purée
2 pounds fresh okra, sliced
1 tablespoon beef base
1 teaspoon Worcestershire sauce
1 cup sherry
3 pounds potatoes, peeled and diced
cornstarch

Heat the oil in a large Dutch oven. Brown the stew meat with the herbs and garlic. Add the remaining ingredients, except the cornstarch, and cover with water. Bring to a boil, reduce heat, and simmer for at least 3 hours. Adjust seasonings to taste and thicken with cornstarch.

Chef Jonathan Lundy, formerly of Jonathan at Gratz Park, a restaurant in the Gratz Park Inn (open from 1998 to 2014), wrote *Jonathan's Bluegrass Table: Redefining Kentucky Cuisine*. Lundy included a new version of burgoo, from which the following is developed, that is very much in the spirit of the original dish but is modernized for today's lifestyle and takes into account modern tastes.[22] One of the benefits of this recipe is that one can complete it in a short amount of time utilizing leftovers.

Jonathan's Kentucky Burgoo

8–12 servings

1 tablespoon olive oil
2 cups onions, diced
1 cup celery, diced
1 cup carrots, peeled and diced
½ cup green peppers, diced
2 cups shiitake mushrooms, sliced
½ teaspoon garlic, minced
¼ teaspoon dried sage
½ teaspoon dried thyme
12-ounce bottle Kentucky ale or dark ale of your choice
½ gallon brown beef stock
2 cups braised bison brisket, cut into bite-size pieces
2 cups roasted pork loin, cut into bite-size pieces
2 cups roasted beef tenderloin, cut into bite-size pieces
½ cup fresh roasted corn, cut off the cob
½ cup frozen soybeans—edamame—or lima beans
¼ cup canned tomatoes, chopped
salt and freshly ground pepper to taste

In a large soup pot, preheat the oil on high heat and sauté the onions, celery, carrots, and peppers for 3–4 minutes.

Add the mushrooms, garlic, and dried herbs. Sauté for 3–4 minutes more.

Add the Kentucky ale. Reduce heat to a simmer. Cook for about 5 minutes to allow alcohol to cook off.

Add remainder of ingredients and simmer for about 20 minutes before serving.

This dish can be made 2–3 days ahead of time and reheated.

ꙮ

Deirdre A. Scaggs and Andrew W. McGraw in their book *The Historic Kentucky Kitchen: Traditional Recipes for Today's Cook* introduce a recipe for Nannie Clay McDowell's burgoo from 1882, stating, "There are few dishes as synonymous with Kentucky as burgoo"; they further acknowledge, "Many recipes call for the inclusion of meats such as squirrel, opossum, and game birds," and they explain that the original recipe in question did in fact call for "chicken, a piece of beef, or any meat that you like." However, to modernize the burgoo recipe, they present one that calls only for chicken—which could be taken as a statement that chicken is most likely what modern consumers have in their refrigerator or freezer at home or are most likely willing to consume. Scaggs and McGraw suggest that more seasoning such as "garlic, Worcestershire sauce, or apple cider vinegar would add greater depth of flavor to the final dish," pointing out that the original recipe did not include any seasoning at all.[23] They also state that they use frozen vegetables—which most people today would use—although in 1882 cooks would not have had access to a home refrigerator, as they were invented in 1913. This recipe for chicken burgoo is based on McDowell's version.

Chicken Burgoo

6–8 servings

1 (3–4 pound) chicken
16 cups cold water
2 tablespoons salt
1 teaspoon black pepper
7–10 new potatoes
1 (28-ounce) can tomatoes, diced
2 cups corn

2 cups okra
2 cups peas
2 cups butter beans or lima beans
4 cups cabbage, chopped

Place the chicken in a large pot, cover with cold water, add the salt and pepper, and bring the water to a boil. Reduce the heat and allow the chicken to simmer until cooked through, roughly 1½ hours. Remove the chicken and allow it to cool. Add the potatoes and tomatoes to the pot and let them simmer until the potatoes are tender, 15–20 minutes. Add the corn, okra, peas, beans, and cabbage and allow them to simmer an additional 15 minutes, stirring frequently. Meanwhile, remove the meat from the chicken. Check the vegetables to make sure they are cooked through, and return the chicken to the pot. Add salt and pepper to taste.

One might think that because burgoo is associated with Kentucky and Illinois, it's regionally confined. However, Justin Joyce, Stephan MacIntyre, Ken Carty, and Michael Carty have a chain of restaurants in Vancouver, Canada, that they have named Burgoo. In 2013 they released a cookbook titled *Burgoo: Food for Comfort*. In the book they relate a story in which they ordered a few cans of burgoo from Kentucky, to serve as inspiration for their signature stew. They wrote, "When the package arrived, we easily cooked up one can and tasted it . . . and we promptly put our spoons back down. Let's just say that after researching (and tasting) many versions of burgoo that may have contained mutton . . . or possum . . . or squirrel . . . , we needed to make our own."[24] They suggest planning 7–8 hours of cooking time and serving the burgoo with homemade mashed potatoes or warm biscuits. This Kentucky burgoo is inspired by their recipe.

Kentucky Burgoo

6–8 servings, with leftovers

2 pounds beef chuck, cut into 2-inch cubes
1 pound lamb shoulder, cut into 2-inch cubes
1 small smoked pork hock, wrapped and tied in cheesecloth,
   or ham cut into 1-inch cubes
2 medium white onions, diced
3 or 4 stalks celery, diced
5 or 6 cloves garlic, minced
2 cans (each 19 ounce) diced tomatoes and juice
¼ cup tomato paste
2 cups good quality beef stock
2 tablespoons Worcestershire sauce
2 tablespoons molasses
2 tablespoons red wine vinegar
2 tablespoons brown sugar
large pinch of chili powder
1 tablespoon or more canned chipotle peppers, puréed or
   chopped fine
pinch of thyme
½ small head green cabbage, diced
2 or 3 medium yellow fleshed potatoes, diced
½ cup frozen corn
4 or 5 fresh okra, thinly sliced in rounds
½ cup lima beans
2 or 3 sprigs fresh oregano, leaves only, chopped
2 or 3 sprigs fresh thyme, leaves only
1 bunch fresh parsley, chopped
sea salt and freshly ground black pepper

Place all ingredients except the fresh herbs in a large ovenproof pot or a slow cooker and stir well. Set the heat to the lowest setting (or the oven to 200 degrees F.) and cook, covered, for seven hours until the meat is tender and falling apart. (You can also cook the stew at a high temperature, say 350 degrees F., for 3 hours.)

Remove the lid and stir to break the meat apart. If you are using the pork hock, remove it, discard the cheesecloth, and separate the meat from the bones. Discard the bones, then chop the meat and add it to the stew. If the vegetables are not yet cooked or the stew is not yet thick, continue cooking the stew uncovered for a little longer. Remove from the heat, stir in oregano, thyme, and half of the parsley, and season to taste with the sea salt and the freshly ground black pepper. Serve family style or in individual bowls and garnish with the remaining parsley.

Some people are particular about the food that they eat and will not consider eating anything that they don't deem to be "normal." For them, the following recipe is perfect! This dish is adapted from *The Derby Party Cooking Clinic* by Barbara Harper-Bach. Harper-Bach admits, "I don't like chicken, squirrel or opossum in my burgoo" and refers to burgoo as "just a glorified beef stew, just soupier."[25]

Beef Burgoo

16 servings

4 pounds stew meat, cubed
¼ cup canola oil
2 teaspoons ground thyme
2 teaspoons ground oregano
2 teaspoons ground basil

1½ cups celery, chopped

1½ cups carrots, chopped

2 cups sweet onions, chopped

1 clove garlic, smashed and diced

1 large 28-ounce can whole, peeled tomatoes, squeezed into
   pieces

2 cups frozen corn, off the cob

2 cups frozen peas

14-ounce can tomato paste

1 tablespoon Kitchen Bokay [bouquet]

2 teaspoons Worcestershire sauce

1 cup sherry

4 pounds potatoes, diced

1 small package frozen okra

1 quart beef broth

enough water to cover

2 tablespoons salt

1 teaspoon freshly ground pepper

½ cup flour

2 cups more water

Brown stew meat in the oil on both sides with the onion and garlic. Add remaining ingredients and cover with water and beef broth. Bring to a boil, then turn heat down to a simmer. Cook uncovered for 3 hours. Thicken with a mixture of the flour and water by putting the water in a quart jar, adding the flour, and shaking well until no lumps remain. Add to burgoo and bring to a boil until thickened. Season to taste.

Ann Simpson was a caterer and cake decorator of great renown in Trigg County. When Ann passed away in October 2010, her daughter, Teresa Ann Simpson, started to compile a cookbook of her mother's recipes called *In the Kitchen with Ann*, which was published in 2013. In the many recipes, one can see why Simpson had a great reputation as a caterer. Her recipe for burgoo cuts the time needed to make the stew by using many prepared ingredients yet still seems to keep the spirit of burgoo from western Kentucky. Ronni Lundy writes that in western Kentucky, "burgoo . . . (has) a deep, thick barbecue sauce like broth." This recipe for pork barbecue burgoo is based on Ann's.[26]

Pork Barbecue Burgoo

6–9 servings

1 quart barbecue pork, shredded
1 (15-ounce) can lima beans, drained
1 (15-ounce) can whole kernel corn, drained
1 (15-ounce) can green peas, drained
1 (15-ounce) can black-eyed peas, drained
1 medium onion, finely chopped
3 medium potatoes, peeled and chopped
3 tablespoons tomato paste
½ teaspoon hot sauce, or to taste
1 teaspoon sugar
1 teaspoon salt
1 teaspoon pepper

Stir all ingredients together in a large pot. Add enough water to make mixture soupy. Simmer on low until potatoes are done. Stir burgoo often to ensure that the mixture is not sticking. Add water while cooking if needed. Stir in sugar, salt, and pepper to taste.

Burgoo has changed over the years, from a thick soup to a thickened stew, from one that always contained squirrel to one that contains beef and chicken (even though USDA-approved squirrel is available), from one that contained fresh vegetables to one that contains frozen or canned vegetables, from one that was usually a large batch that could feed an army to one that feeds a small family. The importance of burgoo is highlighted by the fact that there is a "burgoo belt," which means that burgoo is not really available in most areas. There is no reigning "king" of burgoo, suggesting that burgoo has lost importance in Kentucky or at the very least that no one cares to claim the vacant throne, and the Kentucky public seems not to know or care that we have lost that monarch.

2

Barbecue

Cuisine is a language that speaks volumes about the people who prepare and eat the food of a dialect. As languages are different, so are cuisines; sometimes the differences are subtle, and other times the differences are acute. Barbecue is a common link between different cuisine languages that most societies speak because most cuisines include some type of barbecue, or meat grilled over an open fire or embers. In the past—and again today—the smoked meat of the open fire flavors the meat for the best barbecue, but as we moved cooking inside over a stove, the word *barbecue* has taken on a different meaning, as displayed in many recipes. In some cases, the meat is replaced with hamburger, which is enrobed in a sauce and then baked in the oven. Wes Berry, author of *The Kentucky BBQ Book*, says, "Well, for some purists, BBQ means meat cooked with wood; for others, say in the Midwest, BBQ means a pork roast smothered in sauce cooked in a crockpot. Apparently, based on the cookbooks (used in the research for this book), Kentucky—that middle ground between the North and South—goes both ways, with restaurants that cook up lots of barbecue with wood and home cooks that goop on the sauces and bake it up in the oven."

Barbecue is available across the United States, but when people talk about barbecue there are differences depending on the region of the country from which the barbecue hails. All barbecue slowly cooks over low heat regardless of the region—thus the saying "low and slow"—this is the common link between the regional dialects of cuisine. Therefore, what is cooked and how it is dressed mark the differences between the styles of barbecue. The two major determining factors regarding barbecue styles then are the meat and the sauce—which is sometimes served on top of the meat and sometimes served on the side, depending on the region. For example, in North Carolina the barbecue is primarily about the vinegar-based sauce, although there are differences depending on what part of the state you happen to visit—in some places you are able to find vinegar-ketchup sauce. In Georgia, Tennessee, and Alabama the sauce is sweet and tomato based, while in South Carolina, meat is served with a selection of four sauces: light tomato-based sauce, heavy tomato-based sauce, mustard-based sauce, and vinegar-based sauce—showing the blend of influences of the states to the north, south, and west. Memphis has tomato-vinegar-based sauce, while Kansas City is known for a multitude of meat including fish and a sweet, tangy, tomato-based sauce. Texas barbecue is all about the beef brisket. Some of these regional styles use dry rubs, while others use different types of wood like hickory and mesquite. However, you can find some style of barbecue in every part of the world—again, barbecue is the common link between cuisine languages. Original Kentucky barbecue is about the meat or mutton, although many of the recipes in this chapter will include other meats and all types of sauces for barbecue.

In Kentucky, a large batch of burgoo serves many people and is followed by (and deserves to be followed by) barbecue that will serve as many people. The first recipe is based on one submitted by C. Leslie Dawson and Leo McMillen, the chairmen of the Hardin County Democratic Pig Roast, to the Women's Auxiliary of the Kentucky Association of Plumbing Heating–Cooling Contractors for the 1984 publication *Kentucky's Winning Recipes.*[1] The tongue-in-cheek instructions include several humorous references, including a "good friend's" donation of the hogs and the fire pit (but to make sure that you don't ask the same friend for both the hogs and the pit) and the overestimate of beer for the recipe because the crew cooking the hogs will drink a case of beer. However, the instructions include practical advice such as having a water hose handy in case the hogs catch fire.

Pork Barbecue

500 servings

2 220-pound hogs, prepared for roasting (head, knees, and skin removed)
1 load of wood, green (½ hickory, ½ sassafras)
1 water hose

Cook for 4 hours at 200 degrees F. Raise temperature gradually to 300 degrees F. Pork should be finished in 18–24 hours. Use a new cotton mop to baste the pigs with the basting mixture every ½ hour.

Basting mixture

3 cases cheap beer
2 gallons white vinegar
6 boxes Lipton Onion Soup mix
4 bottles Worcestershire sauce
1 quart lemon juice
salt
pepper
cayenne pepper

Mix 2 cases of the beer with the vinegar, soup mix, Worcestershire sauce, and lemon juice. Season to taste.

Owensboro is sometimes called the "BBQ capital of the world." During the second weekend in May, Owensboro hosts the International Bar-B-Q Festival and competition. This festival features mutton and burgoo among other items for guests to try. The Junior League of Owensboro, Kentucky, authored *To Market, To Market,* which features a pig with a purse riding on a horse on the cover, and on the back cover the same pig riding back from the market holding a full sack of groceries and the words "Home again, home again." This book was inducted into the *Southern Living* Hall of Fame in 1993 and features many recipes, including a recipe for barbecued mutton that includes instructions on how to build a pit to barbecue the mutton.[2] The following recipe is adapted from the Junior League's book.

Daviess County Barbecued Mutton

1 butchered sheep

Barbecue sauce

1 gallon Worcestershire sauce
1 gallon vinegar
1 dozen lemons, sliced
4 pounds lard
4 pounds margarine
¼ pound pickling spice
12 ounces hot sauce
4 ounces black pepper
1 cup salt
6 ounces garlic powder
6 ounces onion powder
2 quarts ketchup

Parboil the sheep for 4 hours in large vats or kettles.

Mix all the sauce ingredients together in a large pot. Bring to a low boil. Reduce heat and simmer for 1 hour or until the lemons are cooked.

Remove the meat from the kettles and place it on a metal wire rack over the barbecue pit.

Baste the mutton generously and frequently with barbecue sauce. Continue to baste each time the meat is turned. The meat should smoke on the pit for 6–8 hours.

❦

Western Kentucky is known for barbecue. This recipe for barbecue sauce is adapted from the book *Sample West Kentucky: A Restaurant Guide with Menus and Recipes* edited by Paula Cunningham.[3]

Lake Barkley Barbecue Sauce

½ cup onion, finely chopped
vegetable oil
2 quarts ketchup or tomato sauce or tomato purée
3 ounces Worcestershire sauce
⅓ small bottle Tabasco sauce
½ pound brown sugar
¼ cup lemon juice
1 tablespoon liquid smoke
1 cup apple cider vinegar
poultry, beef, or pork meat

Sauté onions in small amount of vegetable oil. Add ketchup, Worcestershire sauce, Tabasco sauce, brown sugar, lemon juice, liquid smoke, and vinegar and mix well. Simmer approximately

30 minutes, stirring frequently. Season meat with the sauce and cook until halfway done. Apply more sauce and complete cooking meat slowly, basting several more times with the sauce.

The Franklinton Baptist Church is located in Pleasureville in Henry County, Kentucky. The church traces its history back to Isaac Malin's founding of the church in 1801, and congregants have enjoyed the sermons of more than sixty-five pastors.[4] The church published a cookbook, *Franklinton Friends and Families*, that includes a recipe for barbecue chicken that can be cooked completely in the oven, similar to the following:

Chicken Barbecue Sauce

1 whole chicken, fryer
½ cup margarine
juice of 1 lemon
1 teaspoon salt
1 teaspoon pepper
1½ tablespoons garlic salt
2 tablespoons Worcestershire sauce

Preheat oven to 450 degrees F.

Melt the margarine with the rest of the ingredients. Let the mixture come to a boil, then remove from heat and use it to baste a cut-up fryer. Place the chicken in a greased baking dish in the oven for 20 minutes. Lower oven temperature to 350 degrees F. Remove the juices from around the chicken; add the rest of the sauce and baste often over the next 40 minutes.

The Queen's Daughters of Louisville was founded in 1915 for Catholic women to participate in good works related to "relief and welfare." In 1969 the organization published a cookbook, *Entertaining the Louisville Way*, to benefit Our Lady's Home for Infants. Charlotte Smith donated the recipe for Derby Sauce for Barbeque.[5] Her barbecue recipe is for the oven and uses an enhanced bottled barbecue sauce. It is updated here.

Derby Barbecue Sauce

2 tablespoons butter
1 medium-sized onion, chopped
2 tablespoons brown sugar
1 tablespoon Worcestershire sauce
2 tablespoons water
¼ cup sweet pickle relish
3 tablespoons vinegar
1 cup bottled barbecue sauce

Sauté onion in butter. Add remaining ingredients and simmer for 15 minutes. Use this sauce to cover chicken cut up for baking.

Adding a marinade to the meat will result in the best flavor, but maximum flavor is not the only benefit. The components of most marinades help to break down the proteins in meat, leaving them more succulent and easier to digest. This recipe, inspired by *Marinades and Rubs: 40 Tantalizing Recipes to Stimulate Your Palette and Add Sparkle to Your Meals!*, utilizes Kentucky's native spirit, bourbon.[6] While this marinade may not be part of the traditional Kentucky heritage, it joins the new guard of recipes.

Bourbon and Herb Marinade

½ cup olive oil
4 tablespoons bourbon
3 tablespoons white wine vinegar
3 cloves garlic
1 small onion, sliced
1 tablespoon Dijon mustard
1 teaspoon fresh oregano leaves
1 teaspoon fresh sage leaves
1 teaspoon fresh rosemary leaves
1 teaspoon fresh thyme leaves

Put all the ingredients in a food processor or blender and process until smooth and combined.

Score the meat, poultry, or fish portions deeply with a sharp knife. Put the prepared meat, poultry, or fish in a shallow nonmetallic dish or plastic food bag and cover with the marinade; turn to coat thoroughly. Cover tightly or seal and place in the refrigerator, turning occasionally, for up to 2 hours before cooking.

Here is a sauce recipe based on one by Sandra Bush from *Cook Book 1982: United Methodist Women* from the First United Methodist Church in Frankfort, Kentucky.[7]

Barbecue Sauce

1¼ cups brown sugar
2½ cups corn oil
1¼ teaspoons salt
¼ cup powdered onion
2½ cups Worcestershire sauce

⅝ cup chili powder
1 sprinkle of garlic powder
1¼ teaspoons black pepper
5 cups vinegar
½ cup powdered mustard
¼ cup Tabasco sauce
¼ cup red pepper

Combine all ingredients in a saucepan, then heat on low to mix ingredients. Store in glass jars in the refrigerator until needed.

The Harvey Browne Memorial Presbyterian Church was founded in 1916 in St. Matthews, Kentucky, which is now part of Louisville Metro area. Parishioners have compiled at least two cookbooks, *Hot Browne* in 1984 and *Hot Browne: A Second Helping* in 2003. The titles are puns that reference both the church and one of Kentucky's most famous dishes, the Hot Brown sandwich. Each book contains recipes for barbecue sauces. *Hot Browne* reveals Barbara Elmer's father's "very secret barbecue sauce," which she did not even share with her husband until they celebrated their twenty-fifth wedding anniversary.[8] Here is a version of the recipe:

Dr. Goepper's Barbecue Sauce

1½ quarts white vinegar
10 ounces Worcestershire sauce
2 teaspoons cayenne pepper
4 dashes paprika
1 cup Burgundy wine (red wine)
8 tablespoons sugar

5 tablespoons salt
1 teaspoon black pepper
½ cup oil

Combine all the ingredients. Use to baste spareribs as they cook long and slowly over charcoal, turning and basting frequently. Sprinkle the ribs with some brown sugar, and then place them in a covered roaster with ½ cup water and ½ cup of sauce; keep in slow oven until ready to serve.

Cynthia Frentz contributed a barbecue sauce recipe, adapted here, to *Hot Browne: A Second Helping*, the second book from the Harvey Browne Memorial Presbyterian Church.[9]

Frentz Barbecue Sauce

1 cup ketchup
1 cup vinegar
1 cup water
½ cup butter
½ cup bacon grease
1 teaspoon Cayenne pepper
1 teaspoon allspice
1 clove garlic, finely chopped

Mix all the ingredients on stovetop in saucepan. Simmer for 20–30 minutes.

In 1972 the *Murray Woman's Club Cookbook* seventh edition was published in time for Christmas. The book includes a recipe for chicken prepared in a brown paper bag.[10] The women in the club are identified by their husband's names, and the book was supported by local business advertising. These details remind us of how times have changed: today, paper bags are in short supply, women are rarely identified by their husband's names, and local businesses don't normally advertise in community cookbooks any more. The following recipe is updated from that cookbook.

Chicken Barbecued in a Brown Paper Bag

4 servings

3 tablespoons ketchup
1 tablespoon lemon juice
1 teaspoon salt
2 tablespoons Worcestershire sauce
2 tablespoons butter
1 teaspoon Cayenne pepper
2 tablespoons vinegar
3 tablespoons brown sugar
1 teaspoon dry mustard
4 tablespoons water
1 teaspoon chili powder
1 teaspoon paprika
1 chicken, cut in pieces

Preheat oven to 500 degrees F. Combine the sauce ingredients. Grease the inside of a heavy paper grocery bag and place it inside a roaster pan. Salt and pepper the chicken pieces, dip each in the sauce, and place in the bag. Pour the remaining sauce over them in the bag. Close the bag with a double fold and secure with a metal clip. Bake uncovered for 50 minutes; then cover the pan and roast for 15 minutes longer. Serve extra sauce in a separate bowl.

If you are in need of a kosher recipe for barbecue, here is one adapted from the *Keneseth Israel Sisterhood Cookbook* for chuck roast.[11]

Barbecue Roast

6–8 servings

1 teaspoon concentrated chicken soup mix
3 tablespoons flour
½ teaspoon salt
¼ teaspoon dry mustard
2 cups boiled water
¼ teaspoon pepper
¼ cup Worcestershire sauce
¼ cup vinegar
1 onion, diced
¼ cup ketchup
5-pound brisket roast

Preheat oven to 425 degrees F. Mix all sauce ingredients in a saucepan and bring to a boil. Simmer for 10 minutes. Place brisket in oven for 15 minutes to sear. Reduce heat to 325 degrees F. and continue roasting the meat for about 2 hours, until half done. Pour the sauce over the brisket or chuck roast and continue roasting in the oven for 1 hour or until tender.

The official song of Kentucky is "My Old Kentucky Home," which Stephen Collins Foster composed after a visit to Federal Hill in Bardstown, Kentucky. *My Old Kentucky Homes Cookbook* features a recipe similar to the following for barbecue sauce and ribs.[12]

Barbecue Ribs and Barbecue Sauce

2–4 servings

2 full racks of ribs
salt
pepper
liquid smoke

Sauce

1½ cups ketchup
½ cup vinegar
1 large onion, chopped
2 tablespoons brown sugar
dash Tabasco sauce
1 teaspoon mustard
½ teaspoon salt
¼ teaspoon black pepper

Cut ribs into serving pieces, place on a rack in a broiler pan, and salt and pepper. Place under the broiler and brown on both sides, taking away a lot of the grease.

Mix all sauce ingredients in a pot and cook for about 7 minutes. When the ribs are nice and brown sprinkle them with liquid smoke, place them in a crockpot, and pour the barbecue sauce over them. Set the dial at low and cook for 12 hours.

Capital Eating in Kentucky was published by the American Cancer Society. The following recipe is based on that cookbook's recipe for spareribs.[13]

Easy Barbecued Spareribs

8–10 servings

3 pounds spareribs
1 14–ounce bottle of ketchup
1¼ cup vinegar
3 tablespoons brown sugar
3 tablespoons Worcestershire sauce
1 tablespoon dry mustard
2 teaspoons chili powder
pinch of cloves
pinch of garlic powder

Preheat the oven to 400 degrees F.

Cut the spareribs into serving pieces, place them in a baking dish, and bake for 30 minutes.

Combine the remaining ingredients in bowl; mix well. Pour the sauce over ribs. Reduce the oven temperature to 350 degrees F. and continue baking for another 1½ hours or until tender.

Even though the Ohio River is a natural border on the northern side of Kentucky, some culinary influences do cross the border. *The Cincinnati Cook Book*, which was published in 1967 to benefit the Episcopal Children's Hospital, features a recipe for barbecue sauce that inspired the following.[14]

Barbecue Sauce

1 teaspoon cornstarch
1 can frozen pineapple or orange juice concentrate, or Hawaiian
    punch concentrate

⅓ cup prepared barbecue sauce
⅓ cup brown sugar
1 tablespoon oil
1 teaspoon salt
1 teaspoon onion, chopped
spareribs

Blend the cornstarch and juice concentrate in a pan over low heat. Add the barbecue sauce, brown sugar, oil, salt, and onion and bring to a boil.

Reduce heat and simmer for 5 minutes.

Brush the spareribs liberally with the sauce and grill for about 15 minutes.

❦

The Hodgenville Women's Club produced *Larue County Kitchens of Kentucky* to celebrate the US bicentennial in 1976.[15] This recipe using hamburger is adapted from one of the club's recipes.

Barbecued Beef Patties

4–6 servings

1½ pounds hamburger
1 cup evaporated milk
1½ teaspoons salt
¾ cup quick oats
3 tablespoons onion, diced
¼ teaspoon black pepper
4½ tablespoons shortening

Mix together the hamburger, milk, salt, oats, onion, and pepper and make into patties or balls. Fry them slowly in the shortening until they are brown on both sides.

Sauce

1 tablespoon vinegar
1 cup tomato ketchup
6 tablespoons onion, chopped
2 tablespoons sugar
½ cup water

Combine all the sauce ingredients over a low heat. Place hamburger patties/balls in the sauce and simmer for 30–40 minutes until cooked down low.

A Taste from Back Home by Barbara Wortham features her Aunt Melva's special shredded Bar-B-Q, from which the following is adapted.[16]

Shredded Barbecue

8–10 servings

3–3½ pounds beef or pork, simmered slowly until tender enough to shred with a fork (can use hamburger instead)

Sauce

1 medium onion, diced
½ cup celery, chopped
2 tablespoons fat
2 tablespoons brown sugar
2 tablespoons prepared mustard

1 tablespoon Worcestershire sauce
1 cup water
½ cup ketchup
2 tablespoons chili powder
¼ teaspoon Tabasco sauce
1 8-ounce can tomato sauce

Sauté onion and celery in fat. Add the remaining ingredients and mix. Shred the meat and add it to the sauce; simmer until completely saturated.

Stovetop barbecue moves the cooking into the kitchen from outside. This recipe, based on one from *Lebanon Junction's Old Fashion Cookbook,* is for a large group and is simple to prepare.[17]

Barbecue Beef

8–10 servings

3 pounds ground beef
2 onions, cut up
salt

Sauce

1 14-ounce bottle ketchup
1 tablespoon mustard
2 tablespoons Worcestershire sauce
2 or 3 tablespoons brown sugar
1 tablespoon vinegar

Brown and cook the beef and onions together in skillet. Salt to taste.

Combine the sauce ingredients and simmer for 5 minutes. Pour the sauce over the beef and simmer, covered, for about 1 hour.

For those who have smaller families, this recipe for stovetop barbecue beef might be more appropriate. The recipe is adapted from the *Hepburn Avenue Cookbook*, which was compiled for the benefit of the Highland Island Landmark Fund.[18]

Barbecue

2–4 servings

1 pound ground beef
1 teaspoon salt
1 teaspoon celery seed
⅛ cup brown sugar
⅛ cup vinegar (or less)
¼ cup Worcestershire sauce
1 cup ketchup
½ cup water
½ teaspoon mustard
4 tablespoons lemon juice
2 tablespoons butter
1 onion, diced
1 teaspoon chili pepper

Brown the onion in butter; mix in remaining ingredients and simmer for 30 minutes or until the meat is well done. Serve on buns with chips and pickles.

Cooking with Love and Memories, a cookbook compiled by Order of the Eastern Star in Irvine, Kentucky, features Dru's Bar-B-Que, from which the following is adapted:[19]

Dru's Stovetop Barbecue

8–10 servings

3 pounds ground chuck
2 large onions, chopped
1 green pepper, chopped
1 can Original Manwich
1 small bottle ketchup
¼ cup brown sugar
2 tablespoons Worcestershire sauce
2 or 3 shakes Heinz Gourmet Salad Vinegar
salt and pepper to taste

Brown the ground chuck, onions, and pepper. Drain well. Place the meat in a Dutch oven or crockpot and add the remaining ingredients. Cook until the flavors are completely blended. Add more brown sugar if needed.

Sometimes a small amount of portable barbecue is needed. This recipe, based on one in *Heartwarming Recipes* by the Berea Mennonite Church, is perfect for people on the go.[20] You can also personalize it by using your favorite barbecue sauce.

Barbecue

10–12 servings

¾ pound ground beef
2 tablespoons brown sugar
1 tablespoon onion, minced
1 can refrigerated biscuits
¾ cup cheddar cheese, shredded
barbecue sauce to taste

Preheat oven to 400 degrees F.

In a large skillet, brown the beef, and then drain. Add the barbecue sauce, sugar, and onion. Separate the dough into biscuits; place each in an ungreased muffin cup, pressing the dough up the sides to the edge of the cup. Spoon the meat into the cups and bake for 10–15 minutes. Sprinkle with cheese before serving.

3

Sides

The sides on a plate of barbecue might play just a supporting role, but the meal is not complete without them. The sides are usually starch- or vegetable-based and complete the meal. Most people think of potato salad and coleslaw, but macaroni salad, barbecue beans (or pork and beans), macaroni and cheese, and variations of green salad are also very common at a meal of barbecue. You should fix at least two or three sides for your next barbecue, or ask your guests to bring their favorites.

The Kentucky Cookbook from Golden West Publishers is a small cookbook with some classic Kentucky recipes. Golden West Publishers specializes in regional US cookbooks. One of the side dishes included in this cookbook is for German Potato Salad by Nan Plenge of Shepherdsville, Kentucky, on which the following is based.[1]

German Potato Salad

12 servings

6 slices bacon
¼ cup flour
1 cup vinegar
1½ cups water
1½ cups sugar
6 medium potatoes
½ onion, diced
salt and pepper, to taste
celery seed, to taste

Cut the bacon into small pieces and fry in a skillet until well done but not too crisp. Add flour to the bacon and drippings and lightly brown. Add the vinegar, water, and sugar. Let simmer for 30 minutes or more, stirring occasionally. Boil the potatoes for about 20 minutes (do not overcook; potatoes should be soft and cooked but still firm). Peel and slice the potatoes into ¼-inch slices, then place them in a serving bowl and sprinkle with the onion, salt, pepper, and celery seeds. Pour the warm bacon mixture over the top. Serve hot.

Those who like a mayonnaise-based potato salad might try this recipe, adapted from *Welcome Back to Pleasant Hill: More Recipes from the Trustees' House, Pleasant Hill, Kentucky* by Elizabeth Kremer.[2]

Potato Salad

1 quart

6 medium potatoes
2 tablespoons thin French dressing (see just below)
1 tablespoon onions, chopped
¼ cup celery, chopped
1 teaspoon green pepper, chopped
1 egg, hard boiled and chopped (optional)
1 tablespoon pickle relish
½ cup mayonnaise (or more if you prefer)
salt and pepper to taste

Cook the potatoes in their skins. When tender, drain and cool slightly. Peel and dice the potatoes. Add French dressing and toss;

let stand about 1 hour. Add onions, celery, green pepper, egg, and relish and mix well. Stir in salt and pepper to taste. Add mayonnaise. Serve at room temperature or chill.

Thin French dressing

6 tablespoons oil
2 tablespoons vinegar
¼ teaspoon salt
sliver of onion
2 teaspoons lemon juice
1 teaspoon granulated sugar
¼ teaspoon paprika

Put all the ingredients in a dressing bottle and shake well before using.

🐝

The basis for this macaroni salad is a dish from *Recipes for History, Mystery & Southern Cooking: Springhill Plantation Bed and Breakfast & Winery* by Eddie and Carolyn O'Daniel.[3] The mayonnaise gives the salad a smooth texture and creamy flavor.

Macaroni Salad

6–8 servings

1 pound macaroni, cooked
1 green pepper, diced
1 red onion, diced
3 carrots, shredded
½ teaspoon black pepper
1 can sweetened condensed milk

1 cup red vinegar
2 cups mayonnaise
½ cup sugar

Combine the macaroni, pepper, onion, carrots, and black pepper. Mix together the condensed milk, vinegar, mayonnaise, and sugar. Pour the mixture over the macaroni and toss well before serving.

❦

A barbecue is not complete without baked beans. This recipe, based on the *Kosair Cookbook* from 1973, begins with canned pork and beans and then personalizes the canned recipe, something that home cooks can try by adding their favorite ingredients.[4]

Barbecue Beans

6–8 servings

36 ounces canned pork and beans
1 teaspoon dry mustard
½ cup ketchup
¾ cup brown sugar
6 slices bacon, cut into small pieces
1 small onion, chopped

Arrange ingredients in layers (do not stir) as follows: Empty 1 can of beans (half of the total) into a 1½-quart casserole; combine the brown sugar and mustard and sprinkle half of this mixture over the beans. Top with half of the ketchup, onion, and bacon. Layer with the second can of beans and sprinkle with the remaining brown sugar mixture, bacon, and onion. Spread the rest of the ketchup over all. Arrange 3 or 4 additional bacon slices on top if desired; cook, covered, over slow coals about 1 hour, or bake in oven at 300 degrees F. for 4–6 hours.

The Claudia Sanders Dinner House of Shelbyville, Kentucky, Cookbook by Cherry Settle, Tommy Settle, and Edward Klemm Jr. is dedicated to Colonel Harland Sanders and his wife, Claudia. Cherry Settle's Style Dilled Green Beans are described as "the best green beans in the world."[5] The following dish is based on that recipe:

Dilled Green Beans

8–10 servings

2 quarts canned green beans
4 strips bacon, cut into small pieces
1 large onion, sliced very thin
1 tablespoon salt
1 tablespoon dill weed

In a large pot with a tight lid, alternate layers of green beans, onion, and bacon. Sprinkle each layer with salt and dill weed. Add just enough water to keep the beans from sticking. Bring to a boil. Cover and reduce heat to simmer for at least 1 hour.

The Kentucky Center for the Arts earmarked the proceeds from *Center Cuisine* to benefit special-needs children. The cookbook contains Dot Wadell's bean salad recipe, from which the following is adapted.[6]

Four Bean Salad

12 servings

1 16-ounce can green beans, drained and rinsed
1 16-ounce can wax beans, drained and rinsed
1 16-ounce can kidney beans, drained and rinsed
1 16-ounce can lima beans, drained and rinsed
1 medium green pepper, thinly sliced
1 medium onion, thinly sliced and separated into rings

Combine all the ingredients and toss gently. Cover with dressing (see below), cover, and chill for several hours before serving.

Dressing

¾ cup sugar
½ cup vinegar
½ cup salad oil
½ teaspoon salt
1 tablespoon minced parsley
½ teaspoon pepper

Mix all ingredients in a saucepan over low heat, stirring constantly until sugar dissolves. While still hot, pour the dressing over the bean mixture (see above).

Sacred Heart Academy has been part of the Kentucky landscape since it was founded by the Ursuline Sisters in 1877. The purpose of the academy is to provide education for young women in the Louisville area. In 1997 a committee at the school put together *Cooking from the Heart*, a cookbook of more than four hundred recipes, among which is a recipe for a pasta salad, which inspired the following.[7]

Pasta with Fresh Basil, Tomato, and Parmesan

8–10 servings

16 ounces radiatori, farfalle, or penne pasta
½ cup olive oil
¾ cup Parmesan cheese, freshly grated
1½ cups fresh basil, chopped
3 cups very ripe plum tomatoes, chopped
3 tablespoons lemon juice, freshly squeezed
salt
pepper

Cook pasta in 4 quarts of boiling water until al dente. Drain and toss with the oil and lemon juice. Cool to room temperature, occasionally stirring the pasta so it is completely coated. Add the basil, tomatoes, and cheese, and salt and pepper to taste. Mix thoroughly but gently. Garnish with additional basil leaves.

This recipe for corn pudding is based on one from *Cook's Delight*, a cookbook by the Plainview Pre-School.[8] Corn pudding is found in most cookbooks related to Kentucky and Southern cuisine.

Corn Pudding

6 servings

2 cups corn, canned or fresh from the cob
2 eggs

2 tablespoons melted butter or margarine
2 cups milk, scalded
1 medium green pepper, finely chopped (optional)
1 teaspoon salt
⅛ teaspoon pepper

Preheat oven to 350 degrees F.

Beat the eggs until smooth. Add the remaining ingredients, and then pour into a greased baking dish. Set the dish in a pan of hot water and bake until firm, about 1 hour.

A Walking Tour and Cooking Guide of Saint James Court is a book published by the Saint James Court Association in 1976 for the twentieth annual St. James Court Outdoor Art Show. The book includes the recipe St. James—Memphis Tossed Salad from Mrs. B. L. Hargrove, a Tennessee native, who lived in an apartment at the south end of the court in a complex known as Parfett Flats.[9] The following is an adaptation of her recipe:

St. James—Memphis Tossed Salad

8 servings

1⅓ cup carrot, grated
1⅓ cup celery, chopped
1 bunch radishes, sliced
1⅓ cup cabbage, shredded
1 cucumber, diced

Combine all the ingredients, then toss with a favorite dressing.

This recipe, for a cheesy bean and mushroom casserole, is based on one from Jane Jones of Henderson County, Kentucky. Jones shared her Lima Bean and Mushroom Casserole recipe with *Favorite Recipes of Kentucky–Tennessee*.[10]

Lima Bean and Mushroom Casserole

8–10 servings

2 packages frozen lima beans
2½ cups milk
4 tablespoons butter
3 tablespoons flour
½ pound Swiss cheese, grated
3 tablespoons onion, grated
1 small can mushroom stems and pieces
½ cup toasted bread crumbs, panko, or slivered almonds

Preheat oven to 350 degrees F.

Cook the lima beans until tender; drain. In a saucepan over low heat, combine milk, butter, and flour; slowly add cheese and onion until sauce is smooth. Mix in the lima beans, then immediately place the entire mixture in a casserole dish. Top with crumbs or almonds. Bake until finished about 30 minutes.

Sometimes a simple salad is the perfect side for a barbecue dinner. This one has few ingredients but makes up for that simplicity in flavor. This recipe features Kentucky Limestone Bibb, which is similar to Boston Bibb lettuce, and is adapted from *The Cherokee Triangle Olde Time Cookbook*, written by Mary Catherine Kirtley Young in 1975 for the Cherokee Triangle Association.[11]

Hearts of Palm, Avocado, and Lettuce Salad

8–10 servings

2 medium heads of Kentucky Limestone Bibb lettuce
1 ripe avocado, peeled, pitted, and sliced
1 14-ounce can hearts of palm, chilled and sliced
2 tablespoons vinegar
¼ cup olive oil
½ teaspoon salt
dash of pepper

Break the lettuce into bite-size pieces; then add the avocado and hearts of palm. Mix together the vinegar, oil, salt, and pepper; add the dressing to the salad and toss.

Beans are a good side to barbecue. This recipe is based on *The Best from the Blue Grass*, a cookbook published by the Woman's Club of Central Kentucky.[12] With four different types of beans, this casserole has a nice tangy sauce.

Hot Bean Casserole

12 servings

½ pound salt pork or 8 slices bacon
4 large onions, chopped
½ cup brown sugar
½ cup vinegar
1 can green lima beans
1 can white lima beans
1 can kidney beans
1 can pork and beans

Preheat oven to 325 degrees F.

Fry the salt pork or bacon until done. Remove from the skillet, and cook onions in the grease until they are transparent. Add the sugar and vinegar. Drain all the beans (except the pork and beans) and combine; and add the onion to beans along with the meat. Bake in a 2-quart casserole for 1 hour.

Not everyone likes eggplant, but sometimes people enjoy eggplant when it is part of a bigger dish. This recipe for eggplant casserole is adapted from *Fannin Family and Friends Favorite Foods Often Fabulous! Always Fun!* Many other Kentucky cuisine cookbooks have similar dishes.[13]

Eggplant Casserole

8–10 servings

½ cup mushroom soup
⅓ cup mayonnaise
1 egg
onion juice
1 large eggplant, peeled and cubed
¾ cup cracker crumbs
⅓ stick butter, melted, plus ⅓ stick butter, sliced
1 cup sharp cheddar cheese, grated
salt and pepper, to taste

Preheat oven to 350 degrees F.

Boil the eggplant for 7–10 minutes. Drain and season with salt and pepper. Mix the soup, mayonnaise, egg, cheese, onion juice, melted butter, and some of the cracker crumbs with the eggplant. Put into greased 1½-quart casserole. Sprinkle with the remaining crumbs and dot with the remaining butter. Bake for 30 minutes.

❦

Richard Hougen was the author of five cookbooks, including *More Hougen Favorites*.[14] He included a simple dish that combines Kentucky mint and carrots, upon which the following is based:

Minty Fresh Carrots

6–8 servings

1 pound carrots, sliced ¼ inch thick
½ cup butter
1 teaspoon mint leaves, finely chopped
1 teaspoon salt
¼ teaspoon pepper

Cook carrots in boiling salted water. When tender, but not too soft, drain. Add the remaining ingredients. Cook over low heat for 3 minutes to blend seasonings.

❦

This simple salad is inspired by *The Best of Beaumont: A Recipe Collection*, which was compiled by the Beaumont Presbyterian Church. [15] An orange, beet, and spinach salad is perfect for a barbecue meal.

Orange, Beet, and Spinach Salad

6–8 servings

1 8-ounce can beets, drained and cut into julienne strips
6 cups fresh spinach, leaf lettuce, or romaine lettuce, torn in pieces
3 oranges, peeled and thinly sliced
½ medium cucumber, thinly sliced
½ cup bottled low-calorie salad dressing (such as herb vinaigrette
   or Italian)

Top the greens with the beets, oranges, cucumbers, and dressing.
Toss and serve.

❧

The Moonlite Bar-B-Q Inn Inc. is a Kentucky gastronomic land-mark, serving dishes that are tried and true. The garden salad that inspired the following recipe is in both *"Owensboro's Very Famous" Moonlite Bar-B-Q Inn Inc.: Collection of Recipes* and *Family Favorites from Moonlite: Recipes That Founded a Kentucky Tradition.*[16]

Garden Salad

6 servings

2 tomatoes, coarsely chopped
1 cucumber, coarsely chopped
1 bell pepper, coarsely chopped
1 cup onion, chopped
1 cup vinegar
¾ cup sugar
½ teaspoon salt
½ teaspoon pepper

Mix the vegetables together in large bowl. Cover with the sugar, vinegar, salt, and pepper and mix well. Serve immediately, or store in a tightly covered container in the refrigerator for a few days.

❦

Sweet and sour red cabbage is the perfect dish to accompany barbecue. This recipe is adapted from the *Bicentennial Cookbook, 1789–1989, United Presbyterian Church, Lebanon, Kentucky: Favorite Recipes from Our Best Cooks*.[17]

Red Cabbage

4–6 servings

1 quart red cabbage, shredded
4 tablespoons brown sugar
1 cup water
1 teaspoon salt
1 teaspoon pepper
2 sour apples, sliced
5 tablespoons bacon drippings
½ cup cider vinegar
1 tablespoon caraway seeds

Combine all the ingredients in a large pot, and cook over medium heat for 20 minutes or until hot.

❦

People who don't like purple cabbage or who want to have their salad ready to go can make this sauerkraut ahead of time. This recipe is based on a sauerkraut salad found in *Cookbook: Good Food Recipes, First Lutheran Church, Louisville, Kentucky*.[18]

Sauerkraut Salad

4–6 servings

1 No. 2½ can shredded kraut (drained)
1 medium green pepper, chopped fine
1 medium onion, chopped fine
1 cup celery, chopped fine
1 cup sugar
¼ cup salad oil
¼ cup vinegar
salt, to taste

Combine all ingredients. Store in a closed jar in the refrigerator until ready to serve.

If you plan to go to a barbecue or a church picnic, this salad might be a good dish for you to take; after all, who doesn't like bacon? This recipe is adapted from *Heavenly Creations,* a cookbook from St. Paul United Methodist Church in Louisville, Kentucky.[19]

Tomorrow's Salad

6–8 servings

1 head of lettuce, shredded
1 red onion, sliced
1 pound bacon, fried and crumbled
½ head cauliflower, cut into small pieces
1 small can very small peas

Salad dressing

¼ cup sugar
1 cup mayonnaise
⅓ cup Parmesan cheese
salt and pepper, to taste

In a salad container, layer the ingredients as follows: lettuce, onion, bacon, cauliflower, peas. Prepare the salad dressing and pour over the top of the salad. Cover the container and refrigerate overnight. Mix well before serving.

A carrot and raisin salad works well with barbecue—and also takes me back to my childhood, since I always looked for the carrot and raisin salad at the church potlucks. This recipe is based on the *Trigg County Cook Book*.[20]

Carrot and Raisin Salad

6 servings

4 cups carrots, grated
½ cup salad dressing or mayonnaise
2 tablespoons cream
1 cup raisins
1 teaspoon lemon juice
lettuce leaves

Combine the carrots and raisins. Mix the salad dressing, lemon juice, and cream; then pour over the carrots and raisins and toss well. Serve on lettuce.

This simple salad is adapted from Berea's Best.[21] Try mixing up flavors on this salad by using different onions—sweet onions, red onions, and even chopped green onions. The secret to this recipe is the vinegar-based marinade, which is made of equal parts sugar, water, and vinegar.

Cucumber and Onion Salad

6–8 servings

2 large cucumbers, peeled and sliced in rounds
2 medium-sized onions, peeled and sliced in rings
salt and pepper, to taste
⅓ cup sugar
⅓ cup water
⅓ cup vinegar

Combine the cucumber and onion, and then sprinkle with salt and pepper. Mix together the sugar, water, and vinegar; then pour the mixture over the cucumbers and onions. Toss well before serving.

4

Bread

Bread is one of the most basic elements of any cuisine. Try to think of French or Italian cuisine without bread, much less Southern cuisine without biscuits or cornbread. Bread can take many forms and can be made from a plethora of ingredients. Regardless of the composition of the bread, most can be served seamlessly with burgoo and barbecue. The bread can serve as a side, can be broken into burgoo, or can be sliced to hold the barbecue. Here are some of the most common breads, prepared by some of Kentucky's most famous restaurants and cooks.

A former *Louisville Courier-Journal* reporter, Sarah Fritschner is one of the guardians of Kentucky cuisine and the writer of *Sarah Fritschner's Holidays: Menus and Recipes for the Fall Holiday Season*.[1] Fritschner suggests serving cornbread hot or saving it at room temperature for several days to make cornbread dressing. The following is based on her recipe:

Cornbread

4–6 servings

4 tablespoons butter, melted
2¼ cups white cornmeal
¼ cup flour
1¼ teaspoons salt
1 tablespoon baking powder
1 egg
1½ cups milk

Preheat oven to 450 degrees F.

Put the butter in a 9-inch cast-iron skillet or other heavy pan, then place the pan in the oven to melt the butter and heat the pan. Mix the cornmeal with the flour, salt, baking powder, egg, and milk. When the butter is beginning to brown, remove the skillet from the oven and tip it to coat the sides of the pan. Pour the rest of the butter into the batter and stir to mix. Pour batter back into the hot pan and bake for 25 minutes, or until the cornbread is golden brown around the edges.

The Doe Run Inn was built in 1792 near Brandenburg, Kentucky. Mrs. Lucille Brown, former owner of the Doe Run Inn, donated a recipe for cracklin' bread to *Kentucky Hospitality: A 200-Year Tradition*, published by the Kentucky Federation of Women's Clubs. Brown said her grandmother used cracklin's around "hog killing time."[2] Cracklin's were used not only to make cornbread—they were also used to make soap and to feed chickens. This recipe is adapted from Brown's.

Cracklin' Bread

4–6 servings

2 cups cornmeal
6 tablespoons flour
2 teaspoons sugar
1 tablespoon baking powder
2 teaspoons salt
3 eggs, well beaten
1 tablespoon butter
1 cup milk
½ cup cracklin's (crumbled crisp bacon)

Preheat oven to 425 degrees F.

Mix all ingredients together; then pour into a hot, well-greased iron skillet. Bake for about 30 minutes.

In 1971, the Ballard High School PTA, in Louisville, created a cookbook as a fundraiser. *What's Bruin': Ballard High School Cook Book* includes a recipe from Mrs. Mitchell Nasser for Angel Biscuits—leavened with both yeast and baking powder.[3] The following is based on her recipe:

Angel Biscuits

6 dozen

5 cups all-purpose flour
¾ cup vegetable shortening
1 teaspoon baking soda
1 teaspoon salt
3 teaspoons baking powder
3 tablespoons sugar
1 yeast cake (1 packet of yeast) dissolved in ½ cup lukewarm water
2 cups buttermilk

Sift dry ingredients together; cut in shortening until mixed thoroughly. Add buttermilk and dissolved yeast. Work together with a large spoon until the flour mixture is completely moistened. Cover and put in the refrigerator until ready to use.

When ready, preheat the oven to 400 degrees F. Take out as much batter as needed; roll it onto a floured board to ½-inch thickness and cut into rounds or squares. Bake on a greased cookie sheet or in a round 8-inch or 9-inch cake pan for 12 minutes, or until brown.

❦

The Woman's Hospital Auxiliary from Woodford County released a cookbook in the late 1950s and 1960s that included a recipe for Beaten Biscuits.[4] Here is an updated version.

Kentucky Beaten Biscuits

2 dozen

4 cups flour
1 teaspoon salt
1 teaspoon baking powder
2 teaspoons sugar
½ cup lard
½ cup milk
½ cup cold water

Preheat oven to 325 degrees F.

Combine all ingredients, working them together until the dough blisters. Roll out the dough and cut out the biscuits. Bake on a lightly greased baking sheet until lightly brown on top.

❦

When properly made, biscuits are a thing of beauty and can be the crowning addition to a meal. *The Crowning Recipes of Kentucky* included a buttermilk biscuit recipe by Madonna Smith Echols, who served as Miss Kentucky in 1946.[5] The following recipe is adapted from Echols's.

Buttermilk Biscuits

15 biscuits

4 cups all-purpose flour
2 tablespoons baking powder
1 teaspoon baking soda
1 tablespoon sugar
⅔ cup margarine, softened
1½ cups buttermilk
¼ cup margarine, melted

Preheat oven to 450 degrees F.

Combine the dry ingredients; cut in the margarine and buttermilk, stirring until the dry ingredients are moistened. Turn dough onto a lightly floured surface and knead 4 or 5 times. Roll out the dough and cut with a biscuit cutter. Place the biscuits on a lightly greased baking sheet; brush the tops with melted butter. Bake for about 15 minutes until lightly browned.

Cornbread and a glass of buttermilk used to serve as an afternoon snack. Mush biscuits are similar to cornbread. In *Hillbilly Cookin 2*, Sam Carson and A. W. Vick suggest replacing the cornbread with a mush biscuit to go with the glass of buttermilk.[6] Here is a similar recipe for mush biscuits.

Mush Biscuits

1 dozen biscuits

1 quart hot water
cornmeal
1 cup yeast
1 cup potato water
1 cup lard

1 cup sugar
⅛ teaspoon salt
flour

Combine the cornmeal with the hot water until mushy. Dissolve the yeast in the potato water. Mix the mush and the yeast water with all the other ingredients, adding enough flour to make dough. Let the dough rise in a warm place, and when it doubles its size, roll it out and cut it into biscuits. Bake in a moderate (350 degrees F.) oven until golden brown.

What do you do with leftover cornbread? Consider making pancakes! Kentucky native Ronni Lundy suggests this use for leftover cornbread in her book *Shuck Beans, Stack Cakes, and Honest Fried Chicken: The Heart and Soul of Southern Country Kitchens.*[7] Lundy was born in Corbin, Kentucky, and grew up near Louisville. She wrote and edited for the *Louisville Courier-Journal* during the 1980s and early 1990s, but her writing appeared in many magazines. This recipe is adapted from her book.

Kentucky Cakes

2–4 servings

1 cup cornbread
1 cup milk
1 cup flour
1 teaspoon salt
1 teaspoon baking powder
2 tablespoons brown sugar
2 eggs

1 tablespoon oil
1 cup buttermilk
fried apples or applesauce
bacon

Break the cornbread into pieces, combine with the milk, and let sit in the refrigerator overnight. In the morning, sift the flour, salt, baking powder, and brown sugar together and then mix in with the cornbread. Beat the eggs, oil, and buttermilk and mix with the cornbread flour. Fry in hot skillet.

Serve with the fried apples on top—or if you're in a hurry, you can heat some natural-style applesauce with brown sugar and use that as a topping.

Variation: Fry 4–6 pieces of bacon really crisp and crumble them into the pancake batter when you add the liquid.

In 2007 Bowling Green Municipal Utilities was celebrating sixty-five years of service to the residents of its city. BGMU has a long-standing tradition of publishing a cookbook to give to its customers. The 2007 version, *BGMU Cookbook 2007*, included a recipe for spicy cornbread that serves as the inspiration for the following.[8]

Chili-Cheese Cornbread

4–6 servings

1 cup yellow cornmeal
1 cup flour
¼ teaspoon salt
1 tablespoon sugar

2 large eggs
1 cup milk
2 tablespoons oil
¾ cup cheddar cheese, grated
1 4-ounce can green chilies, drained and chopped
nonstick cooking spray

Preheat oven to 375 degrees F.

Combine cornmeal, salt, flour, and sugar in a medium-sized bowl; make a well in the center of the mixture. Combine milk, eggs, and oil in a separate bowl, then add this mixture to the dry ingredients, stirring just until moistened. Stir in the green chilies and cheese.

Pour the batter into an 8-inch square baking dish coated with nonstick cooking spray. Bake for 30 minutes or until golden brown.

What if you don't think you can cook? That is the approach that Betty Jane Donahoe takes in her 1972 classic *How to Boil Water*, teaching young brides and brides-to-be how to cook for their husbands. This Louisville cookbook includes tips such as "Remember! You can't COOK from the den watching TV." The title of chapter 1 is "Hamburgers," chapter 2 is "Hot Dogs," and it moves through other foods that increase in complexity until the reader reaches "Odds, Ends and Incidentals." This final chapter includes a recipe for spoonbread, adapted here.[9]

Spoonbread

4–6 servings

1 cup self-rising cornmeal
4 cups milk

2 tablespoons butter
4 eggs, beaten

Preheat oven to 425 degrees F.

In a greased 1½-quart baking dish, beat the four eggs and set aside.

Scald the milk in a double boiler. Gradually stir the meal into the milk until it becomes the consistency of mush; add the butter. Now add this mixture, a very little at a time, to the eggs, stirring constantly. Bake for 45 minutes.

Turn off the oven, add additional butter on top of the loaf, and pop it back in the oven until the butter is melted. Serve immediately.

❦

Tanker's Range presents a spicy twist on spoonbread with Mexican Spoonbread, which is adapted below.[10] *Tanker's Range* is a cookbook published by the Officers' Wives Club at Ft. Knox. The titular "range" refers to the stove in the Tankers' home kitchen.

Mexican Spoonbread

8–10 servings

1 can cream-style corn
¾ cup milk
⅓ cup oil
2 eggs, beaten
1 cup cornmeal
½ teaspoon baking soda
1 teaspoon salt
1½ cup sharp cheddar cheese, grated
1 can green chilies, mashed

Preheat oven to 400 degrees F.

Mix all ingredients except the cheese and chilies. Pour half of the batter into a greased casserole. Spread with chilies and half of the grated cheese. Pour the remaining batter over the chilies; then top with the remaining cheese. Bake for 45 minutes. Let stand a few minutes before serving.

Many residents know Thelma Linton as "the best cook in Harrodsburg." Susanna Thomas documented many of Thelma's recipes in *Thelma's Treasures: The Secret Recipes of "The Best Cook in Harrodsburg."* One of the recipes is Thelma's Rolls, upon which the following recipe is based. Thelma has said that she makes seventeen or eighteen dozen rolls each week because people in the community would call or stop by and pay $1 per dozen.[11]

Thelma's Rolls

16–17 dozen

4 packages rapid-rise yeast
pinch of sugar
2 cups water
4 eggs
1 cup butter
1 cup shortening
2 teaspoons salt
not quite 2 cups sugar
16 cups all-purpose flour
3–4 sticks butter or margarine, melted
additional flour as needed

Put a pinch of sugar in a bowl. Heat the water until about 110 degrees F., and then pour it into the bowl. Add the yeast and stir well, approximately 1 minute, until the yeast is dissolved and bubbles up.

In another bowl, beat the eggs with a mixer until stiff, approximately 5 minutes.

In another bowl, beat the cup of butter, shortening, salt, and the rest of the sugar on medium until the mixture gets really creamy, about 3–5 minutes. Turn the mixer to low speed and add the water-yeast mixture. When that is fully combined, turn the mixer back up slightly and add the stiff eggs. When that is well mixed, turn up the mixer a little more and mix for 30 seconds to 1 minute. Spread the mixture out on a piece of waxed paper or aluminum foil and sift 4 cups of the flour out onto it; mix by hand vigorously for 2 minutes until the flour is well blended. Add the rest of the flour 4 cups at a time, beating vigorously by hand for 2 minutes or so after each addition. When all the flour has been added, beat the dough well by hand. Place in a bowl; brush the top of the dough with softened or melted butter or margarine. Cover the bowl well with foil and let it sit several hours until the dough has doubled in size. Put in the refrigerator overnight.

The next day, melt 3 or 4 sticks of margarine or butter in a saucepan and set aside. Take out about a fifth of the dough and knead it gently and quickly with as little flour as possible. Roll it out to ½-inch thickness and cut with a biscuit cutter. Grease the bottom of a pan with the melted butter. Dip each roll in the rest of the melted butter and place it in the pan so that it lightly touches the other rolls. Continue until pan is filled. Let the rolls sit in the pan for about 3 hours while they rise.

Bake at 375 degrees F. for 15 minutes.

Good things come to those who wait! Nothing is truer when it comes to bread. Allowing time (and a little fermentation) to work its magic on bread makes for memorable dining. Bobbie Smith Bryant writes about many things that take time in her book *Passions of the Black Patch: Cooking and Quilting in Western Kentucky.* One of the recipes that she presents is for sourdough bread, including a recipe for sourdough starter, adapted here.[12]

Sourdough Bread

Sourdough starter

1 envelope yeast
2½ cups warm water
2 cups flour
2 teaspoons salt
1 tablespoon flour

Sprinkle the yeast in ½ cup of the warm water and let stand for 5 minutes. Stir in the remaining 2 cups of warm water, flour, salt, and sugar. Put in a large crock or bowl; starter will bubble to about 4 times its volume. Cover loosely with a towel and let stand in a warm place, 80–90 degrees F., stirring down daily. In 3 or 4 days, the starter is ready to use. As starter is withdrawn from the container, replace it with equal amounts of water and flour; remove at least a little out each week and replace it, even if you do not make any bread at the time. Put the starter in the refrigerator after 4 or 5 hours.

Sourdough bread

1 tablespoon butter, melted
2 cups starter
½ teaspoon baking soda
1 teaspoon sugar

2 cups flour
1 teaspoon salt

Preheat oven to 375 degrees F.

Add the butter to the starter. Add all the other ingredients and stir well, adding enough flour to make a thick dough. Turn out on a board and work in enough additional flour to keep the dough from being sticky. Knead until smooth, put in a greased tin, and allow to double in size. Bake for 30 minutes or until brown.

You can drink bourbon, but you can also eat bourbon. Here is an opportunity to eat your bourbon: bourbon bread. This recipe is inspired by *Derby Entertaining: Traditional Kentucky Recipes,* which was published by McClanahan Publishing House in 2008.[13]

Bourbon Bread

2 loaves

¾ cup raisins
⅓ cup Kentucky bourbon
1¼ cups butter, softened
1½ cups sugar, divided, ½ cup and 1 cup
6 eggs, separated
2¼ cups self-rising flour
1¼ teaspoons vanilla extract
1 cup pecans, coarsely chopped

Soak the raisins in the bourbon for 2 hours (or overnight).

Preheat oven to 350 degrees F.

Drain and reserve the bourbon, adding enough bourbon to

make ⅓ cup. Cream the butter and ½ cup of the sugar until light and fluffy. Add the egg yolks, one at a time, beating well. Add the flour in thirds, alternately, with the bourbon; mix until well blended. Stir in the raisins, vanilla extract, and pecans.

Beat the egg whites until soft peaks form. Add the remaining 1 cup of sugar gradually to the egg whites; beat until stiff. Fold the egg whites into the bread batter.

Line the bottoms of 2 loaf pans with waxed paper. Spoon the batter into the pans. Bake for 1 hour.

The Beaumont Inn in Harrodsburg, Kentucky, has been operating for one hundred years. In 2015 the inn and its owners, the Dedman Family, were honored with a James Beard Award as an American Classic. Duncan Hines said in 1949, "The best eating place in Kentucky: Beaumont Inn at Harrodsburg." Mrs. Irvin Ochsner gave her recipe for corn muffins to the Bethel Evangelical & Reformed Church in St. Matthews, Kentucky (now part of Metro Louisville), for the *Bethel Cookbook;* the recipe, adapted here, is also featured in *Beaumont Inn Special Recipes.*[14]

Beaumont Inn Corn Muffins

10–12 muffins

2 cups cornmeal
1½ cups buttermilk
1 teaspoon salt
1 teaspoon (level) baking soda
1 egg

Preheat oven to 450 degrees F.

Burgoo and cornbread.

Barbecue Ribs and Barbecue Sauce (p. 51) with potato salad and barbecue beans.

Barbecue Beef sliders (p. 55), Carrot and Raisin Salad (p. 74), and potato salad with the "Greatest Kentucky Drink" (p. 97).

Bourbon-and-herb-marinated grilled chicken, Minty Fresh Carrots (p. 70), and corn pudding with a Ginger Ale Highball (p. 98).

Barbecue chicken, Macaroni Salad (p. 61), and Moonlite's Garden Salad (p. 71) with an Old Fashioned (p. 105).

Boone Tavern Cornsticks (p. 91).

Cornbread.

Angel Biscuits (p. 79).

Kentucky Cakes (p. 82) and Kentucky Fog (p. 108).

A selection of pies: Brown Sugar Pie (front, p. 118), "Run for the Roses" Pie (left, p. 115), and John Y. Brown Pie (right, p. 116).

Biscuit Pudding with Bourbon Sauce (p. 117).

A slice of "Run for the Roses" Pie (p. 115).

A slice of Pinto Bean Pie (p. 119).

A slice of John Y. Brown Pie (p. 116).

Original Kentucky Whiskey Cake (p. 135).

Apple Cobbler (p. 133).

Peach Cobbler (p. 132).

Half Moon Fried Pies (p. 122) with apple filling.

Beat the egg slightly and put it into buttermilk; then mix in all the dry ingredients. Pour the batter into muffin tins and bake until done.

Richard Hougen was the manager of the Boone Tavern Hotel of Berea College and the author of several cookbooks, including *Look No Further: A Cookbook of Favorite Recipes from Boone Tavern Hotel, Berea College, Kentucky.* Hougen includes the recipe for Boone Tavern Cornsticks. He notes at the bottom of the recipe, adapted here, how important it is to "heat well-greased cornstick pan to smoking hot on top of the stove before pouring in your batter."[15]

Boone Tavern Cornsticks

1 dozen large cornsticks

2 cups white cornmeal
½ cup flour
2 eggs, well beaten
1 teaspoon baking powder
½ teaspoon baking soda
2 cups buttermilk
½ teaspoon salt
4 tablespoons lard, melted

Preheat oven to 450–500 degrees F.
Sift the flour, cornmeal, salt, and baking powder together. Mix the baking soda with the buttermilk, and then add to the dry ingredients; beat well. Add the eggs and beat. Add the lard. Mix well. Pour the batter into very hot well-greased cornstick pans on top of stove, filling the pans to level. Place pans on the lower shelf

of the oven and bake for 8 minutes. Move the pans to the upper shelf and bake for an additional 5–10 minutes.

Martha Layne Collins, Kentucky's first female governor, was elected in 1983. She had already served as lieutenant governor with Governor John Y. Brown. Later she would serve as president of St. Catherine's College in Springfield, Kentucky. As the lieutenant governor, Collins contributed a spoonbread recipe, adapted below, to *Cooking with Middletown Woman's Club.*[16]

Spoonbread with Bourbon

6 servings

2 cups water, boiling
1 cup cornmeal
½ teaspoon salt
2 teaspoons sugar
3 egg yolks, beaten
3 egg whites, stiffly beaten
1 cup buttermilk
4 tablespoons butter
½ teaspoon baking soda
2 tablespoons lard
1 tablespoon bourbon

Preheat oven to 325 degrees F.

Boil the water; add the lard and butter; to this mixture add the cornmeal, egg yolks, and baking soda. Stir in the buttermilk and stiffly beaten egg whites. Add the bourbon and pour into a buttered casserole dish. Bake for 35 minutes.

The Louisville Collegiate School celebrated seventy-five years in 1990. It also published the *Louisville Collegiate School 75th Anniversary (1915–1990) Cookbook*. Included was a recipe for corn fritters, which inspired the following.[17]

Corn Fritters

6–8 servings

2½ cups fresh corn or canned cream-style corn
1 egg yolk, well beaten
2 teaspoons flour
¼ teaspoon salt
1 egg white

Mix together the corn, egg yolk, flour, and salt. Whip the egg white until stiff, but not dry. Fold the egg white into the corn mixture. Into a hot buttered skillet, drop the batter as for pancakes and sauté until light brown and fluffy.

If you are not happy with regular spoonbread, you might try this "souped-up" version, based on *Cooking through the Years with Bullitt County Homemakers*.[18]

Super Spoonbread

8–10 servings

1 can condensed cheddar cheese soup
¾ cup milk

¼ cup butter, melted
½ cup cornmeal
3 eggs, separated
½ teaspoon salt
¼ teaspoon baking powder

Preheat oven to 350 degrees F.

Bring soup and milk together to a boil. Lower the heat and stir in the other ingredients except the egg whites. Whip the egg whites until stiff; then fold them into the batter. Pour into a baking pan and bake for 1 hour.

When people think of cooking with a beverage in Kentucky, most people think of bourbon, but beer has been used for much longer. Beer is a good substitute for milk in any recipe. Beer bread is an easy-to-produce and wonderful addition to a meal. Some suggest the addition of fresh or dried dill weed, "to taste."[19]

Beer Bread

8–10 servings

3 cups self-rising flour
2–3 tablespoons sugar
1 can (12 ounces) beer

Preheat oven to 350 degrees F.

Mix the ingredients with a spoon in a large bowl. Pour the batter into a loaf pan. Bake for 45 minutes.

If time is limited, you might try planning ahead by making this biscuit mix well before you need to serve. If so, you can still claim the biscuits are "homemade" and that they are "something that you just threw together," and you will be completely truthful. This recipe comes from *Southern Bread Winners*.[20]

Quick Biscuit Mix

10 cups mix

8 cups all-purpose flour
2 teaspoons salt
3 tablespoons sugar
5 tablespoons baking powder
2 teaspoons cream of tartar
2 cups shortening

Sift the dry ingredients together. Cut in the shortening with a pastry blender or food processor until it resembles coarse meal. Store in a tightly covered container. Does not require refrigeration.

To use the quick biscuit mix, take:

2 cups of the quick biscuit mix
½–⅔ cup milk

Preheat oven to 450 degrees F.
    Combine the ingredients to form a soft dough. Start with ½ cup milk and use only the amount needed to moisten the mix. Roll and cut the biscuits and place on a baking sheet. Bake for 10 minutes or until golden brown.

5

Bourbon

Bourbon is hard to find in Kentucky cookbooks—outside of bourbon balls, which seem to be in almost every cookbook. The reason that few cookbooks use bourbon, especially as a beverage, is that many of the counties in Kentucky are still dry. In older texts this translates into very few, if any, bourbon drinks recorded in the literature. Here are some drinks that were found during my research, adapted and updated as necessary.

Sometimes simple is best. That is the case with this first recipe for a bourbon-based drink, which was adapted from the original recipe featured in *Cooking with Bourbon*. The original recipe says that this drink is good for "30 minutes of sipping pleasure."[1] One of the benefits of this drink is that the water opens up the bourbon, allowing the consumer to enjoy the flavor of the whiskey.

"The Greatest Kentucky Drink"

an Old Fashioned glass or a tumbler
3 ice cubes
2 ounces Kentucky bourbon
4 ounces branch water

Place the ice cubes into the tumbler. Add the bourbon and branch water.

🦃

If you decide to add something to your bourbon, you might consider ginger ale. The ginger ale highball is a simple drink but clearly a popular part of Kentucky cuisine. However, Irvin S. Cobb wrote, "Personally, I dislike to see the taste of fine whiskey sullied by ginger ale."[2]

Ginger Ale Highball

a highball glass
ice
2½ ounces bourbon
ginger ale

Fill the highball glass halfway with cracked ice. Add the bourbon. Fill the glass with ginger ale.

The South is known for mint juleps. The mint julep is part of Kentucky's cuisine because of the famous horse race, the Kentucky Derby; however, these are the premade bottled juleps. While the julep may be associated with the horse race, in fact, "it is part and parcel of Kentucky lore and of Kentucky social life and hospitality," dating from the time when Kentucky was part of the Commonwealth of Virginia. The mint julep can be a strong drink that can be hard to resist; one author suggests the drinker say, "Get thee behind me, Satan," in order to resist. Some have suggested that the whiskey is optional. Others have suggested that "the nectar of the Gods is tame beside" the mint julep and that "the bourbon and the mint are lovers." The best juleps in the world are said to be made at the Pendennis Club in Louisville, which "requires that the mint not be crushed." When making the mint julep, one should use only good Kentucky bourbon, which some people consider to be "liquid joy." This recipe is adapted from Paducah's own Irvin S. Cobb.[3]

Mint Julep

Put 12 sprigs of fresh spearmint in a bowl, covered with powdered sugar and just enough water to dissolve the sugar, and crush the leaves with a wooden pestle. Place half the crushed mint and liquid in the bottom of a crackled glass tumbler, or in a sterling silver or pewter tankard. Fill the glass half full with finely crushed ice. Add the rest of the crushed mint and fill the remainder of glass with crushed ice. Pour in Four Roses or Paul Jones Whiskey until the glass is brimming. Place in the refrigerator for at least 1 hour (preferably 2–3 hours—if you can wait that long). Decorate with sprigs of mint covered with powdered sugar when ready to serve.

The Moon Glow is an original drink found in *Hospitality: Kentucky Style* by Colonel Michael Edward Masters. Colonel Masters says this drink "finds favor with the gentlewomen."[4]

Moon Glow

crushed ice
1½ ounces bourbon
2 ounces cranberry juice
2 ounces orange juice
2 teaspoons maraschino cherry juice

Pack a tall glass with crushed ice. Add the cranberry juice and the orange juice. Add the maraschino cherry juice. Then add the bourbon. Stir well with a bar spoon and garnish with 2 maraschino cherries and a straw.

The employees of the electric company in Louisville produced a cookbook, *Somethin's Cookin at LG&E,* and included a bourbon punch.[5]

Bourbon Punch

15–20 servings

1 large can pink lemonade concentrate, undiluted
1 64-ounce bottle 7-Up or lemon-lime soda
1 jar maraschino cherries
1 cup (80-proof) bourbon

Mix all ingredients in large bowl. Freeze. Serve when slushy.

There are many bourbon slush recipes. This one comes from *A. Lincoln Legacy Tasting Tour.*[6]

Bourbon Slush

10–12 servings

2 cups strong tea
1 cup sugar
1 12-ounce can frozen lemonade (as is)
1 6-ounce can frozen orange juice
6 cups water
1½ cups bourbon
1 orange slice
1 maraschino cherry
1 sprig mint

Mix all of the liquid/frozen ingredients with the sugar. Freeze at least 12 hours. Remove from freezer 1 hour before serving. Scrape into a glass while still icy. Serve with straw and top with the orange slice, maraschino cherry, and sprig of mint.

Captain (Retired) Henry E. Bernstein of the US Navy invented the Bourbaree, which was featured in Tom Hoge's *The Bourbon Cookbook*.[7] With all due respect to Captain Bernstein, the honey disperses better in the drink if it is cut with warm water.

Bourbaree

2 cocktails

1 ounce lime juice
1 ounce honey
½ ounce hot water
3 ounces bourbon
dash bitters
6 ice cubes

Cut the honey with the water, then mix all the ingredients in a blender. Pour into cocktail glasses.

The Kentucky Toddy is listed in *The Mixicologist* by Chris F. Lawlor, who in 1895 was the "chief bartender" at the Burnet House in Cincinnati and was formerly the chief bartender at the Grand Hotel. In addition to alcoholic drink recipes, the book has chapters on "Temperance Drinks," the "Don'ts for Young Bartenders," and "The Model Bartender." The book also has a chapter on "Health and Alcohol," which cites a study by the British Medical

Association. The study's results listed the lifespan of five classes of people based on a study of more than four thousand people.[8]

Class	Lifespan
Total abstainers	51 years 1 month
Moderate drinkers	63 years ½ month
Occasional drinkers	59 years 2 months
Habitual drinkers	57 years 2 months
Drunkards	53 years ½ month

The book contains two drinks that are similar, the Kentucky Toddy and the Old Fashioned Toddy.[9]

Old Fashioned Toddy

1 lump sugar
water
1 ice cube
1 jigger whiskey
dash nutmeg
a thick glass

Dissolve the sugar in a little water, the ice, and the whiskey; stir. Add the nutmeg, and serve in the same glass.

The Kentucky Toddy

Same as Old Fashioned Toddy, adding a little lemon peel to the drink before serving.

This next drink, Old Kentucky Toddy, comes from a book called *Here's How*, which was published in 1941 in North Carolina. The wood cover on the book makes it unique. After the directions, in parentheses, the author suggests to readers that this drink will transport them back in time: "And prepare to dream of the good old days, 'befo de war.'"[10] Please note the addition of peach brandy and the substitution of an orange peel for the lemon peel in the Kentucky Toddy. Also, by 1941 the Kentucky Toddy was considered "old."

Old Kentucky Toddy

silver goblet or large toddy glass
ice cubes
1 teaspoon granulated sugar
water
whiskey
1 teaspoon peach brandy
1 curl orange peel

Fill the glass ⅔ full of ice; add the sugar, dissolved in a small amount of water. Stir until the glass frosts; then almost fill with choice of whiskey. Add the peach brandy, and top with the orange peel.

When you have a crowd of people—perhaps with the barbecue on the grill—a good solution to satisfy everyone's thirst while waiting for food would be a punch, something easy to fix for a large crew at once.

Excellent Bourbon Punch

16 10-ounce drinks

1 pint iced tea
1 pint pineapple juice
1 quart orange juice
1 pint lemon juice
1 quart ginger ale
1 pint bourbon
2 cups sugar
1 pint water

Boil the water and sugar for at least 3 minutes. Allow the resulting simple syrup to cool. Stir in the rest of the ingredients. Serve chilled.

Kentucky Kitchens, Volume II: I Hear You Calling Me includes a whiskey sour punch recipe by Sandy Adams.[11]

Whiskey Sour Punch

25 servings

1 small orange
3 6-ounce cans frozen lemonade concentrate, thawed
3 cups orange juice, chilled
1 32-ounce bottle club soda, chilled
2 trays ice cubes
1 fifth bourbon

Cut the orange into thin slices, discarding the end pieces. Flute the edges of each slice with a small sharp knife; set aside. Combine the lemonade, orange juice, club soda, ice cubes, and bourbon in a punch bowl; mix well. Garnish with orange slices.

Members of Louisville's Pendennis Club have long claimed the Old Fashioned Whiskey Cocktail as their own. The Pendennis Old Fashioned features muddled fruit, but other establishments choose not to muddle the fruit. Whiskey Ambassador Bernie Lubbers, who is also known as the "Whiskey Professor," offers a traditional Pendennis-style Old Fashioned in his book *Bourbon Whiskey Our Native Spirit: Sour Mash and Sweet Adventures.*[12]

Old Fashioned

slice of orange cut in a half moon
cherry
splash water
2–3 dashes of bitters
small lump or cube sugar
ice cubes
soda water
shot bourbon

In a lowball glass, add a cherry, the orange slice, a sugar cube, the bitters, and a splash of water. Muddle the contents; then add a shot of bourbon and ice, and top off the glass with soda water.

One of Kentucky's favorite fall sweet treats is the bourbon ball— the kind that you eat. Bartender Joy Perrine took that idea and converted it into a drink, the bourbonball, one of her many award-winning cocktails. Perrine and Susan Reigler featured this drink in their book *The Kentucky Bourbon Cocktail Book.*[13]

Bourbonball

1 part bourbon
1 part Tuaca
1 part dark crème de cacao
1 strawberry

Combine the ingredients; shake over ice, and strain into a chilled glass. Garnish with a strawberry on the rim.

The sidecar is a classic cocktail that combines three ingredients that balance one another for the perfectly flavored drink. While the original sidecar contains brandy, this one contains bourbon.

Bourbon Side Car

1½ ounce bourbon
¾ ounce Cointreau
¾ ounce lemon juice, fresh squeezed
sugar

Fill a Boston shaker with ice; add bourbon, Cointreau, and lemon juice. Close the shaker and shake until you hear the ice beginning to change. Strain into a chilled cocktail glass with a sugar rim. (Hint: You can set the sugar rim on the cocktail glass hours in advance, and then place in a freezer to chill the glass and set the sugar.)

Perhaps the most classic late-fall drink is eggnog. Sandy Talbott contributed this eggnog recipe to the Junior League of Louisville, which published *CordonBluegrass: Blue Ribbon Recipes from Kentucky*.[14] Talbott advises, "You cannot overbeat the egg yolk, sugar, bourbon and rum. They must be beaten well to keep the eggnog from separating," and, "This eggnog is better if made 2–4 days ahead."

Bardstown Talbott Eggnog

15–20 servings

12 large eggs, separated
1 cup granulated sugar
1 quart good Kentucky bourbon whiskey
1 cup good light rum
1 quart coffee cream
1 quart whipping cream, whipped
freshly grated nutmeg, for garnish

Add the sugar to the unbeaten egg yolks and beat on high speed with an electric mixer until the mixture is light and smooth. Add the bourbon, a little at a time, beating on high. Add the rum, and beat again thoroughly.

In a separate bowl, beat the egg whites stiff and fold them into the mixture above. Add the coffee cream, and fold in the whipped cream. Refrigerate. Sprinkle the top with nutmeg before serving.

The Cooking Book by the Junior League of Louisville included this hot bourbon drink, which is perfect for late fall.[15]

Kentucky Mocha

2 heaping teaspoons Suisse Mocha or hot chocolate mix
2 tablespoons water, boiling

1½ ounces bourbon
hot water
whipped cream

Dissolve the Suisse Mocha or hot chocolate mix in boiling water. Add the bourbon plus the hot water to fill the cup ¾ full. Stir and top with whipped cream.

❦

In the fall, fog begins to cover the ground in the early morning. This next recipe is a good change for people who are tired of eggnog. The formula for this drink is listed in many Kentucky-area cookbooks including *Festive Firsts*, where it is called "Bourbon Fog"; *Bellarmine Designers' Show House Cookbook* and *The Cincinnati Cook Book*, both of which list their recipes under the name "London Fog"; and an ice cream–heavy version in *In the Kitchen with Ann* called "coffee freeze."[16]

Kentucky Fog

12 servings

1 quart Kentucky bourbon
1 quart strong coffee
1 quart vanilla ice cream

Combine the ingredients in a punch bowl and serve.

❦

Hasenour's Restaurant was a Louisville culinary landmark for more than sixty years. The Hot Tom and Jerry was its signature drink and is the only beverage recipe in *Hasenour's: The History of a Louisville Restaurant Tradition*.[17]

Hot Tom and Jerry

1 egg, separated
1 cup superfine granulated sugar
pinch of baking soda
1 ounce rum
hot milk
1½ ounce Maker's Mark whiskey
brandy
nutmeg

Beat the egg white until frothy. Beat the egg yolk thoroughly. Combine the white and the yolk. Add enough superfine sugar to stiffen the egg mixture. Add to this a pinch of baking soda and ½ ounce of the rum to preserve the batter. Add a little more sugar to stiffen (about ¼ cup).

To serve: In a warm mug dissolve 1 tablespoon of the batter in 3 tablespoons of hot milk. Add the whiskey; then fill the mug with hot milk to within ¼ inch of the top. Stir. Top with a touch of brandy, a sprinkle of nutmeg, and a little more rum.

Everyone in the South knows about eggnog, but boiled custard is something unique to Kentucky. Many recipes for boiled custard don't include bourbon, but this one from *Love Is . . . #2 in Your Collection of "Breckinridge Co. Homemakers" Recipes* includes Kentucky's finest spirit.[18]

Boiled Custard

8–10 servings

6 eggs

3 cups sugar
2 quarts milk
1 quart bourbon
1½ tablespoons butter, melted
1 tablespoon vanilla
1 pint heavy cream, whipped

Beat the eggs; add the sugar and milk. Cook in a saucepan over low heat until the mixture coats a spoon. Stir in the vanilla and butter. Strain, and then add to the whipped cream. Add the bourbon and serve.

Tailgating is a fall activity that happens before football games. In the late fall as the weather cools, having something warm to drink is important. *In Kentucky TALEgating II: More Stories with Sauce,* Kelli Oakley and Jayna Oakley offer up an apple cider spiked with bourbon.[19]

Bourbon-Spiked Apple Cider

20 servings

two 64-ounce bottles apple cider
2 tablespoons packed dark brown sugar
4 whole cloves
½ cup orange juice
2 tablespoons fresh lemon juice
¼ teaspoon ground all-spice
4 cinnamon sticks, broken in half
1½ cups bourbon

Mix all the ingredients except the bourbon in a large pot. Bring to a boil over high heat. Reduce the heat to medium and simmer until the mixture is reduced by one quarter (or about 12 cups), about 30 minutes. Using a slotted spoon, remove the cinnamon and cloves. Add the bourbon. Ladle into cups.

6

Desserts

Of the many suggestions for finishing a meal that begins with burgoo, pie is most often mentioned. The base of almost every pie is the crust, which seems to be a sticking point for the home cook. Many cookbooks contain a recipe for "no-fail" piecrust. Shirley Corriher, CCP, shares her expertise on making a piecrust in *CookWise: The Hows & Whys of Successful Cooking with Over 230 Great-Tasting Recipes*. Corriher writes that the basic formula for piecrust is 1–3; "one part fat to three parts flour (by volume)."[1] Corriher spends almost fourteen pages of her book on how to make the perfect piecrust, discussing different ingredients and techniques. Here is an adaptation of Corriher's recipe:

Piecrust

1 cup bleached all-purpose flour (national brand)
½ cup instant flour (such as Wondra or Shake and Blend)
Or
1½ cups pastry flour or low-protein flour

¼ teaspoon salt
8 tablespoons unsalted butter, cut into ½-inch cubes
2 tablespoons shortening or lard

Combine the flour, salt, butter, and lard, working together by hand until the dough has a smooth consistency. Refrigerate until ready to roll out for piecrust, at least 1 hour.

Or you can try:

Maggie Green's All-Butter Crust

½ cup butter, cut into 1-inch slices
1½ cups unbleached all-purpose flour
1 teaspoon sugar
½ teaspoon salt
3–4 tablespoons ice water

Place the butter in the freezer to chill. Meanwhile, blend the flour, sugar, and salt in a food processor with a medal blade. Add the butter and pulse the processor on and off until the butter is the size of large peas. With the processor running, drizzle in the water. Stop processing when the dough begins to form a ball. Do not overmix. Place the dough onto a large piece of plastic wrap. Fold the plastic wrap over and around the dough to seal, and press the dough into the shape of a disk. Refrigerate for at least one hour.

After the dough has chilled, unwrap and place it on a lightly floured surface. Roll it into an 11-inch circle and place the dough into a 9-inch pie pan. To flute the edge, use the index finger on one hand to push the dough between the thumb and index finger of the other hand, forming U-shaped indentations about 1 inch apart around the entire edge. Refrigerate until ready to fill.[2]

The real recipe for Derby Pie® is a well-guarded secret, known by only a few people. Derby Pie® is a trademarked title for a pie made by the Kern's Kitchen Corp. There are many pretenders but only one real deal. The names of the pretenders include "Favorite Louisville Pie," "Winning Ticket Pie," "Oldham Pie," and "Run for the Roses Pie."[3]

One of the pretenders, "Run for the Roses," won the 1976 Kentucky State Fair; it is updated as follows.[4]

"Run for the Roses" Pie

8 servings

¼ cup margarine, melted
1 cup sugar
3 eggs
¾ cup light corn syrup
¼ teaspoon salt
1 teaspoon vanilla
½ cup chocolate chips
½ cup English walnuts, chopped
2 tablespoons Kentucky bourbon, plus a little extra

Preheat oven to 375 degrees F.

Soak the walnuts in 2 tablespoons bourbon and set aside. In a mixing bowl, beat the margarine, sugar, and eggs with a spoon until fluffy. Blend in the corn syrup, salt, and vanilla. Add the chocolate chips. Take strainer and drain walnuts, reserving the bourbon. Add the walnuts to filling mixture. Add new bourbon to the reserved portion to bring the quantity back to 2 tablespoons. Add the bourbon to the filling mixture and blend well. Pour into a partially baked crust and bake for 55 minutes. Use either a homemade or purchased (frozen) 9-inch piecrust; prick bottom and sides and bake 7 minutes at 350° F. Cool.

An adaptation similar to Derby Pie® is a pie named after a former governor of Kentucky. John Y. Brown Jr. was the fifty-fifth governor of Kentucky and is the ex-husband of Phyllis George, a former Miss America. He is the son of former US congressman John Y. Brown Sr. and the father of former Kentucky secretary of state John Y. Brown III. Brown is also the former part-owner of Kentucky Fried Chicken (KFC).

Patti's 1880's Restaurant, located in Grand Rivers, Kentucky, is famous for thick charbroiled pork chops and "mile high" meringue pies; it is also home to the John Y. Brown Pie, which was made in honor of Governor Brown's trip to the restaurant. This recipe, adapted here, is featured in both *Miss Patti's Cook Book* and *Sample West Kentucky: A Restaurant Guide with Menus and Recipes.*[5]

John Y. Brown Pie

8 servings

1 cup sugar
½ cup flour
½ cup butter, melted
2 eggs, slightly beaten
4 ounces butterscotch chips
1 cup pecan pieces
1 teaspoon vanilla
1 9-inch unbaked pie shell

Preheat oven to 325 degrees F.

Mix together the sugar and flour. Add the butter and blend well. Stir in the eggs, chips, nuts, and vanilla. Pour the pie filling into the pie shell. Bake for 1 hour or until golden brown. Pie will wiggle when done and set as it cools.

There are two restaurants that claim this recipe for Biscuit Pudding with Bourbon Sauce. The first is Kurtz Restaurant in Bardstown, and the second is the Science Hill Inn in Shelbyville.[6] Here is one version.

Biscuit Pudding with Bourbon Sauce

8–10 servings

10 1½-inch biscuits
1 quart milk
6 eggs
2 cups sugar
2 tablespoons vanilla
2 tablespoons butter, melted
bourbon sauce (see below)

Preheat oven to 350 degrees F.

Break the biscuits into small pieces in a large bowl. Add the milk; soak 5 minutes. Beat the eggs with the sugar and vanilla and add to the biscuit mixture. Pour the butter into a 2-quart baking dish, add the pudding, and bake until set, about 1 hour. Serve warm with bourbon sauce.

Bourbon Sauce

1 stick butter
1 cup sugar
1 egg
⅓ cup bourbon

Melt the butter in a heavy pan. Add the sugar and cook for 5 minutes, stirring occasionally. Beat the egg in bowl, gradually adding the butter mixture while whisking constantly. Add the bourbon and mix well.

ꙮ

Brown sugar pie is one of Kentucky's and the South's quintessential desserts. It is served with and without meringue. This recipe comes from Mary Addie Freeman, who donated the recipe to the *College Hill United Methodist Church Cookbook*, which was published in 1989. College Hill United Methodist Church is located in Waco, Kentucky, which is in Madison County. The book was loaned to me by a sixth-generation Kentuckian, Lauren Gold, with whom I worked at Sullivan University. Amber Nate updated and tested this recipe at the Bakery on the Sullivan University campus in Louisville.

Brown Sugar Pie

8 servings

3 eggs
1 pound light brown sugar
1 stick (4 ounces) butter, melted
2 pinches salt
1 tablespoon bourbon
1 piecrust

Preheat oven to 350 degrees F.

Prepare a pie pan with the piecrust.

Whisk together the eggs and add in the sugar, butter, salt, and bourbon. Whisk together until combined well and smooth. Pour into the piecrust.

Bake for 45 minutes or until golden brown. Check to see that the pie is baked through—it will be gooey, but it should be set all the way through.

Pinto beans in a dessert pie may go against the normal idea of a way to end a meal. However, Pinto Bean Pie is listed in *Cooking through the Years with Bullitt County Homemakers, From the Kitchens of Barren County Homemakers, Still Cookin' after All These Years: The Presidents Club of South-Central Kentucky,* and *Cooking with Middletown Women's Club.* The "poor man's pecan pie" found in *Cookin' from Scratch: Taylor County Homemakers* also features pinto beans. This is an original recipe based on the idea of using pinto beans for a dessert pie.[7]

Pinto Bean Pie

8 servings

2½ cups freshly cooked pinto beans, puréed
½ teaspoon allspice
½ teaspoon nutmeg
¼ teaspoon cloves
¾ cup sorghum
½ cup sugar
2 eggs
1 teaspoon vanilla
1 piecrust, partly baked

Soak the pinto beans overnight or for at least 8 hours.

Preheat oven to 350 degrees F.

Boil the pinto beans until they are soft, drain the water, then purée the beans. In a separate bowl add the three spices, sorghum, sugar, and eggs and mix together. Add the mixture to the puréed pinto beans and combine until the consistency is smooth. Add the vanilla and incorporate into the mixture. Pour the pie filling into the piecrust. Bake for 35–40 minutes.

🌿

Before Chef Edward Lee became notable for his appearance on Bravo's *Top Chef,* he directed the kitchens at 610 Magnolia. Nancy Miller's *Secrets of Louisville Chefs Cookbook, Volume Two: More than 225 Great Recipes Plus Cooking Tips from the Chefs* featured a recipe for mint julep ice cream from Chef Lee, adapted as follows:

Mint Julep Ice Cream with Bourbon Sauce

About 1 quart

Bourbon sauce

½ cup high-quality bourbon
⅓ cup of sugar

Ice cream

1 cup high-quality bourbon
½ cup sugar
2 cups milk
20 stems fresh mint
6 large egg yolks

Garnish

fresh berries
tiny sprigs of mint

Bourbon sauce: Combine the bourbon and sugar in a heavy-bottom pot and heat over a medium flame. Be cautious as the bourbon may ignite. When the liquid comes to a boil, turn the heat to low and allow to simmer for 15 minutes. Turn the heat off, transfer the syrup to a container, and chill for at least 1 hour. The syrup will stay fresh in an airtight container in the refrigerator for a couple of months.

Ice cream: Combine the bourbon and sugar in a heavy-bottom pot and heat over a medium flame. When the liquid comes to a boil, turn the heat to low and allow to simmer for 15 minutes. Reserve warm.

Warm the milk in a heavy-bottom pot until it just comes to a simmer. Turn off the heat, add the mint, and let the flavor infuse for at least 1 hour at room temperature. Strain, discard the mint, and reserve warm.

Combine the bourbon syrup and the mint-flavored milk and stir well.

Whisk the egg yolks until pale, about 2 minutes. Gradually drizzle the warm milk and bourbon liquid into the eggs until all the liquid is smoothly combined with the yolks. Refrigerate this mixture and chill for at least 1 hour or overnight.

Use the mixture to make ice cream according to your ice cream maker's instructions. Chill for 1 hour. Scoop the ice cream into a bowl and drizzle a little bourbon syrup over it. If desired, garnish with fresh berries and tiny sprigs of mint. Serve immediately.

❦

Chess Pie is a classic dessert served in the Commonwealth of Kentucky. This recipe is based on *Kentucky Always in Season* by Greta Hipp Burkhart. Burkhart suggests serving the pie "warm or if refrigerated, served chilled with a dollop of whipped topping and a sprinkle of nutmeg."[8]

Commonwealth Chess Pie

8 servings

3 egg yolks
1 cup of milk
¾ cup sugar
½ cup margarine
2 tablespoons all-purpose flour
1 teaspoon vanilla
1 9-inch baked pie shell

Combine the egg yolks, milk, sugar, margarine, flour, and vanilla in the top of a double boiler. Bring the water in the boiler to a boil, constantly stirring the top pan. When the mixture begins to thicken to a custard consistency, turn the heat off. Continue to stir for 2 minutes, then allow to set for 5 minutes. Pour the custard into the baked pie shell.

This recipe for fried pies was first mentioned in *Kentucky Hospitality*, a 1976 publication of the Kentucky Federation of Women's Clubs, and then later in the 1998 publication *Smokehouse Ham, Spoon Bread & Scuppernong Wine: The Folklore and Art of Southern Appalachian Cooking* by Joseph E. Dabney. The recipe is credited to Mrs. Earle Combs of Richmond, Kentucky. A similar recipe is found in *A Slice of Kentucky: Sharing Our Recipes*, with more spices including nutmeg, allspice, and cloves.[9]

Half Moon Fried Pies

16 miniature pies

1 pound dried apples or peaches
¾ cup sugar
2 tablespoons butter or margarine

2 teaspoons cinnamon (to taste)
piecrust
lard
additional sugar

Cover the dried fruit in water and soak overnight. Drain the fruit, add a small amount of fresh water, and cook slowly until tender. Mash the fruit. Add the sugar, butter or margarine, and cinnamon. Stir well and let the mixture cool.

Make your favorite piecrust, using only half the regular amount of shortening. Cut into circles 4–6 inches in diameter. Place a generous tablespoon of the fruit filling on one side of each circle. Fold the other side over and seal firmly along the edge with your fingertips or a fork. Fry in about ½ inch of hot lard, turning once. When the pastry is browned, remove and drain on paper towels. While the pies are still warm, sprinkle them lightly with sugar.

Alternatively, bake the pies at 400 degree F. for about 30 minutes; brush the top with melted butter before baking in order to make the surface crisp.

The recipe for Amber Pie is based on *Favorite Fare II,* which was published by the Woman's Club of Louisville in 1984. The book includes a section titled "Kentucky's Favorite Food," which includes classics such as Henry Bain Sauce, Cissy Gregg's Kentucky Burgoo, and the Hot Brown, to name a few.[10] Amber Pie is located in this section; however, there are few references to this pie in other books.

Amber Pie

8 servings

2 eggs
2 teaspoons flour
½ cup sugar
¼ teaspoon salt
½ cup sour cream
1 teaspoon lemon extract
2 tablespoons buttermilk
1 cup blackberry jam
2 tablespoons butter, melted
1 unbaked 9-inch pie shell

Preheat oven to 400 degrees F.

Beat the eggs and set aside. Stir the other ingredients (except the pie shell) together well; then beat in the eggs. Pour the filling into the pie shell and bake until the crust is brown. Reduce the oven temperature to 350 degrees F. and bake for 30 more minutes.

Similar to brown sugar pie, Kentucky Pie is based on a brown-sugar mixture. *Favorite Fare* by the Woman's Club of Louisville featured the recipe from which the following was adapted.[11]

Kentucky Pie

8 servings

1 unbaked rich 9-inch piecrust
½ cup butter
3 cups brown sugar
5 eggs
½ cup light cream
1 teaspoon vanilla

⅛ teaspoon salt
1 tablespoon cornmeal

Preheat oven to 450 degrees F.

Cream the butter, sugar, and eggs together. Add the rest of ingredients. Pour the filling into the piecrust and bake for 5 minutes. Reduce heat to 325 degree F. and bake for another 45 minutes until firm. Cool on cake rack and serve warm.

Kentucky Tombstone Pudding is mentioned in *Charles Patteson's Kentucky Cooking* and in *The Farmington Cookbook*. Patteson suggests serving a pudding such as this in the fall around Halloween, perfect for the traditional burgoo season.[12]

Kentucky Tombstone Pudding

8 servings

6 egg yolks
1 cup sugar
1 teaspoon flour
1 cup dessert sherry (e.g., PX sherry)
2 dozen almond macaroons
2 egg whites
pinch salt
pinch cream of tartar
2 tablespoons sugar
½ cup whole almonds

Preheat oven to 300 degrees F.

Beat the yolks until thick and lemon colored. Mix 1 cup of

sugar and the flour together, and then beat the mixture into the yolks. Add the sherry and cook over low heat, stirring constantly, until thickened. Pour the custard over macaroons that have been arranged in a shallow, ovenproof baking dish.

Add the cream of tartar and salt to the egg whites. Beat until stiff, gradually adding the sugar. Beat until the sugar is dissolved. Spread over the custard, covering it completely. Stud with almonds (to represent tombstones), and bake until lightly browned, about 15 minutes. Serve hot.

The Blue Grass Cookbook includes two recipes for Transparent Pie.[13]

Transparent Pie

16 servings

Number 1

8 egg yolks
½ pound butter
1 pound sugar
1 wineglass wine, flavored with lemon
2 9-inch piecrusts

Preheat oven to 350 degrees F.

Mix the eggs yolks, butter, sugar, and wine together. Pour into the piecrusts and bake for 30 minutes.

Number 2

4 eggs, separated
1 cup butter

2 cups sugar
2 tablespoons blackberry or raspberry jelly
1 9-inch piecrust

Preheat oven to 350 degrees F.

Beat the sugar and butter. Beat the egg yolks until smooth; add in the sugar and butter mixture and continue beating until smooth. Mix in the jelly. Pour into the piecrust and bake for 30 minutes.

Beat the egg whites until they peak; use them as a meringue for the pie once it has cooled.

🌶

Marion Flexner included a recipe for Transparent Pie in her classic *Out of Kentucky Kitchens*. The modern cook might also try this recipe adapted from *Mountain Recipe Collection* by Valeria S. Ison.

Transparent Pie

8 servings

1 tablespoon vanilla
1 heaping tablespoon flour
6 tablespoons milk
¾ teaspoon salt
3 tablespoons water
1 cup sugar
3 egg yolks
2 tablespoons heaping butter, melted
1 9-inch piecrust

Preheat oven to 350 degrees F.

Cream the sugar and butter together. Add the milk, water, eggs, and vanilla. Then add the salt and flour. Beat well, then pour into piecrust. Bake for 1 hour.

☙

Woodford Pudding is named for Woodford County, Kentucky. This outstanding pudding is found in almost every Kentucky cuisine cookbook. This version comes from *We Make You Kindly Welcome* by Elizabeth Kremer and is featured in the book *Kentucky's Best: Fifty Years of Great Recipes* by Linda Allison-Lewis. Lewis adds the vanilla sauce, which she sourced from Kremer's book.[14] *The Larue County Kitchens of Kentucky* was published in 1976 by the Hodgenville Woman's Club. The cookbook contains three recipes for Woodford Pudding, each with a different sauce. I have included the three sauces with an adapted pudding recipe: Nutmeg Sauce, Butterscotch Sauce, and Bourbon Sauce.

Woodford Pudding

6–8 servings

½ cup butter
1 cup flour
1 teaspoon baking soda
1 teaspoon cinnamon
1 cup sugar
1 cup blackberry jam
½ cup sour milk
3 eggs

Preheat oven to 375 degrees F.

Mix all the ingredients together well. Bake in a pudding dish for 40 minutes or until lightly firm.

Vanilla Sauce (for Spice Puddings)

½ cup sugar
1 tablespoon cornstarch
1 cup water, boiling
1 teaspoon vanilla extract
2 tablespoons vanilla bean seeds
few grains nutmeg
few grains salt

Mix the sugar and cornstarch. Gradually add to the boiling water and boil for 5 minutes. Remove from the heat and add the other ingredients. Serve hot.

Nutmeg Sauce

½ cup sugar
1 tablespoon cornstarch
¼ teaspoon salt
freshly grated nutmeg
1 cup water
2 tablespoons butter
½ teaspoon pure vanilla extract

To avoid lumps, first mix the sugar and cornstarch in a saucepan over low heat. Add the water and salt. Cook until the mixture is clear and thick. Mix in the butter, vanilla, and nutmeg to taste. Serve hot over warm pudding.

Butterscotch Sauce

1½ cups dark brown sugar
4 tablespoons flour

1 cup water, boiling
dash salt
4 tablespoons butter
2 tablespoons cream
½ teaspoon vanilla extract

In a saucepan over low heat, mix the dark brown sugar and flour;
then add the water and salt. Stir and cook for 6–8 minutes. Remove from the stove and add the butter, cream, and vanilla. Blend
well and keep warm until used.

Bourbon Sauce

½ cup sugar
1 whole egg
1 tablespoon flour
1 pint water, boiling
2–3 tablespoons good bourbon

Beat the sugar and egg together. Add the flour, then the boiling
water. Flavor with the bourbon. Serve over pudding.

In 1982 the Kentucky division of the American Cancer Society
published a cookbook, *Partytime in Kentucky*. Connie Martin
from Williamstown in Grant County donated a recipe for a traditional Kentucky jam cake, updated here.[15]

Traditional Jam Cake

2 cups all-purpose flour
2 tablespoons baking soda
1 teaspoon salt

1 teaspoon ground cinnamon
1 teaspoon ground nutmeg
1 teaspoon ground cloves
2 cups sugar
1 cup vegetable oil
3 eggs, beaten
1 small jar prune baby food
½ cup blackberry jam
1 cup buttermilk
2 tablespoons pecans, chopped

Preheat oven to 350 degrees F.

Sift together the flour, baking soda, salt, cinnamon, nutmeg, and cloves, 3 times over waxed paper; set aside.

Combine the sugar, oil, and eggs; mix well. Stir in the prunes and jam, mixing well. Add the dry ingredients, mixing well. Stir in the buttermilk and pecans until blended. Pour the batter into a greased and floured 10-inch tube pan. Bake for 30–35 minutes.

Let cool slightly; then remove from pan. When cake is cool, frost with caramel icing.

Caramel Icing

1 cup firmly packed brown sugar
½ cup sugar
½ cup milk
¼ cup butter
1 tablespoon light corn syrup
1 teaspoon vanilla extract

Combine all ingredients in a saucepan over low heat; stir well. Heat to a rolling boil; cook for 1 minute. Let cool completely at room temperature, and then use to frost the cake. Note: if the icing mixture is too thin, add a small amount of powdered sugar until the desired consistency is achieved.

In 1971 the Woman's Auxiliary to the Jefferson County Medical Society published *Prescriptions for Cooks, Volume II.* Mrs. William E. Hopkins donated a peach cobbler recipe to the project; it is adapted as follows.[16]

Peach Cobbler

8–10 servings

1 No. 2½ can peach halves (about 3½ cups)
1½ cups sugar
½ cup milk
1 teaspoon baking powder
4 tablespoons butter
1 cup plus 1 tablespoon flour
¾ teaspoon salt
1 cup juice (of the canned peaches)

Preheat oven to 325 degrees F.

Arrange the peach halves in the bottom of a deep baking dish; reserve the peach juice.

Mix together ¾ cup of the sugar; the milk, baking powder, and butter; 1 cup of the flour; and ½ teaspoon of the salt. Pour this batter over the peaches.

Mix ¾ cup of the sugar, 1 tablespoon of the flour, and ¼ teaspoon of the salt; sift this mixture over the batter. Pour the juice over the top. Bake for 1 hour.

Cook's Delight is a cookbook by Plainview Pre-School in Louisville. It includes a recipe for an Easy Cobbler, which is good for any fruit but in this case is adapted for apples.[17]

Apple Cobbler

8–10 servings

1 stick butter
1 cup flour
2 cups sugar
3 teaspoons baking powder
½ teaspoon salt
1 cup milk
3 cups apples, peeled and sliced
1 cup water
cinnamon, to taste (optional)

Preheat oven to 350 degrees F.

Melt the butter in 9 by 13–inch baking dish. Mix the flour, 1 cup of the sugar, the baking powder, and salt in bowl. Add the milk gradually. Pour the mixture into the baking dish.

Combine the fruit, water, and the remaining sugar. Pour the fruit over the batter; sprinkle with cinnamon if desired. Bake for 45 minutes or until golden brown.

One of the desserts recommended for burgoo is vanilla ice cream.[18] This recipe is based on *Bluegrass Winners*.

Vanilla Ice Cream

2½ quarts

2 cups half-and-half
4 cups milk
12 egg yolks, beaten
2 cups sugar
1 teaspoon salt
4 teaspoons vanilla
1 cup whipping cream (do not whip)

In the top of a double boiler, scald the half-and-half and milk.

Beat the egg yolks well; add the sugar and salt and beat until well blended.

Pour the scalded half-and-half and milk over the egg yolk mixture; return all to the double boiler and cook, stirring constantly, until the mixture coats a metal spoon. Cool.

Put the mixture into a 1-gallon ice cream freezer; add whipping cream and vanilla. Freeze until firm.

People cook with what they have available. When people have great products to cook with, they are able to produce great dishes. So when you come from an area that makes the best whiskey in the world—bourbon—it is only natural that you use bourbon in cooking. Sometimes you can have your cake and eat the bourbon too. This recipe is based on *Derbytown Winners Cookbook*, which was published by the Crescent Hill Woman's Club.[19] The Original Kentucky Whiskey Cake was credited to Mrs. T. G. Stigall.

Original Kentucky Whiskey Cake

15–20 servings

5 cups flour, sifted
1 pound sugar
1 cup brown sugar
¾ pound butter
6 eggs, separated and beaten
1 pint Kentucky bourbon
1 pound candied cherries, cut in pieces
2 teaspoons nutmeg
1 teaspoon baking powder
1 pound shelled pecans
½ pound golden raisins, halved, or ½ pound dates, chopped

Soak cherries and raisins in bourbon overnight.

Preheat oven to 250–275 degrees F.

Cream the butter and sugars until fluffy. Add the egg yolks and beat well. To the butter and egg mixture, add the soaked fruit and the remaining liquid alternately with the flour. Reserve a small amount of flour for the nuts. Add the nutmeg and baking powder. Fold in the beaten egg whites. Add the lightly floured pecans last. Bake in a large greased tube pan that has been lined with 3 layers of greased brown paper. Bake for 3–4 hours. Watch baking time carefully.

Store any leftovers in an airtight container in the refrigerator.

Burkesville, Kentucky, is in southern Kentucky close to the Tennessee border near Lake Cumberland. The town held a bicentennial celebration in 2010 and, as part of the celebration, published *Burkesville, Kentucky, Now and Then, A Bicentennial Celebration:*

200 Years of Treasured Recipes. I was lucky enough to acquire a copy of this cookbook as a gift from the Cumberland County Library Staff when I spoke there in 2010. The book includes a recipe for Sweet Potato Pie, adapted here, that was submitted by Nada Groce from the Spears Chapel Community Church.[20]

Sweet Potato Pie

8 servings

2 eggs, lightly beaten
1 teaspoon salt
1 teaspoon cinnamon
2 tablespoons butter
1 cup sugar
⅛ teaspoon nutmeg
1 cup milk
1½ cups sweet potatoes, mashed
1 9-inch pie shell, unbaked

Preheat oven to 450 degrees F.

Mix together all the ingredients and pour into the unbaked pie shell. Bake for 10 minutes; then reduce oven to 350 degrees F. and bake for 30–40 minutes, or until filling is firm.

Annie Johnson was born in the "Deep South," the daughter of a sharecropper. The Rankin family of Louisville hired Johnson as a cook/housekeeper when Jane Lee Rankin was only six weeks old. Rankin would eventually attend the Culinary Institute of America in New York, graduating with honors. Johnson and Rankin would form a lifelong bond that is outlined in Rankin's book

Cookin' Up a Storm: The Life and Recipes of Annie Johnson.[21] The book has many Kentucky cuisine recipes including spoonbread, Benedictine, barbecue, and many cakes and pies reflecting the heritage and the background of both the author and her friend, the book's subject. One recipe, for pumpkin pie, is adapted here.

Pumpkin Pie

8 servings

1 9-inch piecrust, unbaked
2 cups pumpkin, shredded or canned
½ cup unsalted butter, melted
1 cup sugar
3 eggs, beaten
⅓ cup milk
1 tablespoon all-purpose flour
1 teaspoon cinnamon
1 teaspoon nutmeg
1 teaspoon allspice

Make the 9-inch piecrust (see the recipe on page 113), line the pie pan, and flute the crust.

Preheat oven to 350 degrees F.

In a medium-sized bowl, combine the pumpkin, butter, and sugar and mix well. Add the eggs and milk, mixing well. Stir in the flour and spices until well combined. Pour the mixture into the unbaked piecrust. Bake on the bottom rack for 25–30 minutes, or until the pie is set. Move to the top rack for the last 5 minutes to brown the crust.

The Kentucky Fresh Cookbook by Maggie Green includes a recipe, adapted here, for a single-crust Shaker Lemon Pie. The original Shaker Lemon Pie, which was featured in Elizabeth Kremer's *We Make You Kindly Welcome* and Caroline Piercy's *The Shaker Cookbook*, sports a double crust.[22]

Shaker Lemon Pie

8 servings

1 9-inch all-butter piecrust
2 lemons, washed and carefully sliced paper thin
2 cups sugar
4 eggs

In a bowl, combine the lemons and sugar. Stir well, cover, and let sit for 2 hours.

Preheat oven to 425 degrees F.

Line a 9-inch pie plate with the piecrust (see the recipe on page 114) and place it on a rimmed baking sheet. Add the eggs to the bowl with the lemon and sugar mixture. Pour the batter into the piecrust. Bake for 15 minutes. Reduce the oven temperature to 350 degrees F. and bake for about 40 minutes more, until the pie no longer jiggles in the middle when the pan is gently moved back and forth. Let cool before slicing.

Acknowledgments

The author would like to thank his wife, Kimberly, and sons, Thomas and Michael, for their love and support. Also his parents, Thomas H. and Elizabeth Schmid, and brothers and sisters and their families: Gretchen, Tiffany, Rachel, Justin, Bennett, Ana, Shane, and John.

This book was written, in part, thanks to a Sullivan University faculty grant, which helped to make the research for this project possible. A special note of thanks goes to Dr. Mark Wiljanen, Director of Institutional Research at Sullivan University, for supervising the grant and providing constant support.

I also thank Charles Brown, the Dean of University Librarians at the Sullivan University Library, and his staff, especially Nathan Ragland, for providing immeasurable help in the research for this book.

I feel fortunate to have been helped in recipe execution for the photo shoot by a talented group of staff members and former students at Sullivan University (photo next page).

Jonathan Jeffrey, Professor, Department Head, Manuscripts/Folklife Archives Coordinator, Western Kentucky University: thank you for sharing your library with me, and for supporting and helping with this project.

Dr. Wes Berry, brother and Professor of English at Western Kentucky University and author of *The Kentucky BBQ Book*, and his wife, Elisa, for their friendship and support of this project.

Dr. Andrew McMichael, friend and Associate Professor of History at Western Kentucky University, for your support and friendship.

Dr. Thomas Smith, Professor at Sullivan University, for helping with food styling, and Tammy Logsdon, Assistant Pro-

From left: Jessica Lamb, CWPC; Lejla Alic, CPC; Amber Nate, CPC; Amanda Redemann, CWPC; Lex Padilla; Marissa "Missy" Hill; Robin Richardson, CPC; Albert Schmid, CEC, CCE, CCA, MCFE, CFBE, CHE, CHIA, CCP, COI, CFD, CSS, CSW; Amanda Schiessl; Stephanie Bohnak; KaJaunee "Joy" Davis; Ti'Shonda Pumphrey; and Shayla Clark.

fessor at Sullivan University: I miss working with both of you each day, and I thank you for your support on this project.

Jennifer Gaither, Lauren Gold, Dr. Jeff Johnson, Bob Metry, Quentin Moser, Sarah Nichter, and Derek Spendlove and all the Sullivan University faculty and staff (former and present) members who shared their opinions, expertise, and experience for this book.

David H. Dodd, Allen Akmon, and Rob Beighey, Chairs and Directors of all National Center for Hospitality Studies faculty members, who shared their opinions, expertise, and experience for this book.

Chancellor A. R. Sullivan; President Glenn Sullivan; Dr. Jay Marr, Sullivan University CEO; and Dr. Kenneth Miller, former Provost of Sullivan University: thank you for encouraging and supporting this project.

My new friends and colleagues at Guildford Technical Community College, including L. J. Rush, Linda Beitz, Keith Gardiner, Thomas Lantz, Michele Prairie, Alan Romano, Patrick Sanecki, and Rita King. Also Lisa Knight, Dr. Tom Nevill, and Dr. Randy Parker, president of GTCC: thank you for supporting me.

The author would also like to thank the following musical artists to whom he listened in his office while he wrote this book: Justin Timberlake, the Who, Counting Crows, Gary Allan, Mark Ronson, the Black Eyed Peas, Sergio Mendes, Kid Rock, Keith Urban, and Kentucky natives Chris Stapleton and Alethea Cage.

Notes

1. Burgoo

1. Anne Willan, *Great Cooks and Their Recipes: From Taillevent to Escoffier* (Boston: Little, Brown and Company, 1977, 1992), 89; Sarah R. Labensky and Alan M. Hause, *On Cooking: A Textbook of Culinary Fundamentals,* 2nd edition (Upper Saddle River, NJ: Prentice-Hall, 1995, 1999), 4–5; http://www.telegraph.co.uk/news/worldnews/1353970/Origins-of-first-restaurant-challenged-after-200-years.html; Rebecca L. Spang, *The Invention of the Restaurant: Paris and Modern Gastronomic Culture* (Cambridge, MA: Harvard University Press, 2000), 9.

2. Ronni Lundy, *Shuck Beans, Stack Cakes, and Honest Fried Chicken: The Heart and Soul of Southern Country Kitchens* (New York: The Atlantic Monthly Press, 1991), 135; Justin Joyce and Stephan MacIntyre, *Burgoo: Food for Comfort* (Vancouver, BC: Figure 1 Publishing, 2013), 5; Wes Berry, *The Kentucky Barbecue Book* (Lexington: The University Press of Kentucky, 2013), 168; Daniel Beard, *Camp-Lore and Woodcraft* (Mineola, NY: Dover Publications, Inc., 2006), 119; Staff, *Brighton, Illinois, Centennial Cookbook, Famous for Burgoo Soup, 1869–1969,* Souvenir Edition (Brighton, IL, 1969), 90.

3. Janet Alm Anderson, *A Taste of Kentucky* (Lexington: The University Press of Kentucky, 1986), 21; Charles Patteson with Craig Emerson, *Charles Patteson's Kentucky Cooking* (New York: Harper & Row, 1988), 23, 24; Gene Wallace, *The ABC's of Illinois Festivals: Apples, Burgoo & Cornbread* (Urbana: University of Illinois, 1959), 3; Alben W. Barkley, *That Reminds Me* (Garden City, NY: Doubleday & Company, Inc., 1954), 15; Berry Craig, *True Tales of Old-Time Kentucky Politics: Bombast, Bourbon, and Burgoo* (Charleston, SC: The History Press, 2009), 13, 14; Lillie S. Lustig, S. Claire Sondheim, and Sarah Rensel, *The Southern Cook Book of Fine Old Recipes* (Reading, PA: Culinary Arts Press, 1935), 13, 121; Barbara Harper-Bach, *The Derby Party Cooking Clinic* (n.p.: Barbara Harper-Bach, 2013), 48; Lundy, *Shuck Beans,* 135; James Villas, *Stews, Bogs & Burgoos: Recipes from the Great American Stewpot* (New York: William Morrow and Company, Inc., 1997),

138; Berry, *Kentucky Barbecue Book,* 3, 144, 168; Beard, *Camp-Lore,* 121; Marion Flexner, *Out of Kentucky Kitchens* (New York: Bramhall House, 1949), 45.

4. David Nemec, *The Beer and Whiskey League: The Illustrated History of the American Association—Baseball's Renegade League* (Guilford, CT: The Lyons Press, 2004), 178; Lundy, *Shuck Beans,* 135; Jean Anderson, "Kentucky Burgoo," epicurious.com; James A. Ramage and Andrea S. Watkins, *Kentucky Rising: Democracy, Slavery, and Culture from the Early Republic to the Civil War* (Lexington: University Press of Kentucky, 2011), 171, 282; Robert F. Moss, *Barbecue: The History of an American Institution* (Tuscaloosa: The University of Alabama Press, 2010), 115; Beard, *Camp-Lore,* 119, 121.

5. Nancy and Arthur Hawkins, *The American Regional Cookbook: Recipes from Yesterday and Today for the Modern Cook* (Englewood Cliffs, NJ: Prentice Hall, Inc., 1976), 87; Craig, *True Tales,* 13; *The Farmington Cookbook* (Louisville, KY: Farmington, 1979), 162; Wallace, *ABC's of Illinois Festivals,* 6; Margaret M. Bridwell, *Kentucky Fare: A Recipe Book of Some of Kentucky's Mouth Watering Specialties* (n.p.: Margaret M. Bridwell, 1953), 11–12; Flexner, *Out of Kentucky Kitchens,* 46; Villas, *Stews, Bogs & Burgoos,* 138; *Kentucky Heritage Recipes* (Louisville, KY: Historic Homes Foundation, 1976, 1977, 1978, 1980), 80; Lillian Marshall, *The Courier-Journal & Times Cook Book* (Louisville, KY: The Louisville Courier-Journal & Louisville Times Company, 1971), 91.

6. Minnie C. Fox, *The Blue Grass Cookbook* (Lexington: The University Press of Kentucky, 1904, 2005), 37–38.

7. *The Monterey Cookbook* (Monterey, KY: Cedar Creek Community School, 1986), 9.

8. Staff, *Brighton, Illinois, Centennial Cookbook,* 90; Beard, *Camp-Lore,* 120.

9. Craig, *True Tales,* 14.

10. Lustig, Sondheim, and Rensel, *Southern Cook Book,* 6.

11. Flexner, *Out of Kentucky Kitchens,* 45.

12. Hawkins, *American Regional Cookbook,* 87.

13. Bridwell, *Kentucky Fare,* 5, 12.

14. Linda Allison-Lewis, *Kentucky's Best: Fifty Years of Great Recipes* (Lexington: University Press of Kentucky, 1998), 214–15.

15. John Finley, ed., *The Courier-Journal Kentucky Cookbook* (Louis-

ville, KY: The Courier-Journal and Louisville Times Company, 1985), 50.

16. Marshall, *Courier-Journal & Times Cook Book*, 91; George Washington Ranck, *The History of Lexington, Kentucky* (Cincinnati: Robert Clarke & Co., 1872), 159–60; Cabbage Patch Circle, *Cabbage Patch: Famous Kentucky Recipes* (Louisville, KY: Gateway Press, Inc., 1952, 1954, 1956), 27; Woman's Club of Louisville, *Favorite Fare II* (Louisville, KY: The Woman's Club of Louisville, 1984), 9; Finley, *Courier-Journal Kentucky Cookbook*, 50.

17. Wayne died on December 15, 1796, from complications of gout at Fort Presque Isle in present-day Erie, Pennsylvania, where he was buried. His son Isaac Wayne would follow his father both in the army, eventually serving as a colonel of the Second Regiment, Pennsylvania Volunteer Infantry, and in the 18th Congress, representing Pennsylvania's 4th congressional district. In 1809 Isaac Wayne visited his father's gravesite with the intention of moving General Wayne four hundred miles to St. David's Episcopal Church in Radnor, Pennsylvania. When the coffin was opened, the general was found to be well preserved. However, Isaac did not have enough room to carry his father's body. In a ghastly turn of events, to solve the problem, General Wayne's body was boiled in a large iron kettle until the flesh fell off the bones. The flesh was returned to the grave at the fort while his son carried the bones to St. David's Church, where they are buried. So General Wayne, former congressman and commander in chief of the Army, is buried in two places in Pennsylvania. Legend has it that some of the bones fell from the bags on the way back to St. David's Church and that the general haunts the four-hundred-mile road, looking for his bones.

18. Patteson, *Charles Patteson's Kentucky Cooking*, 25; Moss, *Barbecue*, 118.

19. Jeff Maxwell, *Secrets of the M*A*S*H Mess: The Lost Recipes of Private Igor* (Nashville: Cumberland House, 1997), 116.

20. Villas, *Stews, Bogs & Burgoos*, 111.

21. Sharon Thompson, *Flavors of Kentucky* (Kuttawa, KY: McClanahan Publishing House, 2006), 112–13.

22. Jonathan Lundy, *Jonathan's Bluegrass Table: Redefining Kentucky Cuisine* (Louisville, KY: Butler Books, 2009), 58.

23. Deirdre A. Scaggs and Andrew W. McGraw, *The Historic Ken-*

tucky Kitchen: Traditional Recipes for Today's Cook (Lexington: University Press of Kentucky, 2013), 55–57.

24. Joyce and MacIntyre, *Burgoo,* 93.

25. Harper-Bach, *Derby Party Cooking Clinic,* 48.

26. Teresa Simpson, *In the Kitchen with Ann* (Kearney, NE: Morris Press Cookbooks, 2013), 61; Lundy, *Shuck Beans,* 135. Trigg County is named for Lieutenant Colonel Stephen Trigg, who was an officer in the Revolutionary War and a delegate to the Continental Congress. Colonel Trigg died in 1782 at the Battle of Blue Licks, which happened ten months after the surrender of Lord Charles Cornwallis at Yorktown, when his column was ambushed. Trigg died within the first ten minutes of the battle, and his troops retreated. When the troops returned to recover his body they found Trigg's body mutilated.

2. BARBECUE

1. Women's Auxiliary to the Kentucky Association of Plumbing Heating-Cooling Contractors, *Kentucky's Winning Recipes* (Shawnee Mission, KS: Circulation Service, 1984), 21.

2. *To Market, To Market* (Owensboro, KY: The Junior League of Owensboro, Inc., 1993), 162.

3. Paula Cunningham, ed., *Sample West Kentucky: A Restaurant Guide with Menus and Recipes* (Kuttawa, KY: McClanahan Publishing House, 1985), 105.

4. Jacky Newton, *Franklinton Friends and Families* (Collierville, TN: Fundcraft Publishing, 2005?).

5. The Queen's Daughters, Inc., comp., *Entertaining the Louisville Way* (Louisville, KY: The Queen's Daughters, 1969), v, 59.

6. *Marinades and Rubs: 40 Tantalizing Recipes to Stimulate Your Palette and Add Sparkle to Your Meals!* (Bath, UK: Paragon Books Ltd., 2007), 26.

7. *Cook Book 1982: United Methodist Women* (Lexington, KY: First United Methodist Church, 1982), 89.

8. *Hot Browne: A Second Helping* (Lenexa, KS: Cookbook Publishers, Inc., 2003), ii, 352.

9. *Hot Browne: Second Helping,* 252.

10. Mrs. (Lou Ann) Lawrence Philpot, ed., *Murray Woman's Club Cookbook,* 7th ed. (Nashville: Reed Publishing Company, 1972), 173.

11. Keneseth Israel Sisterhood, *Keneseth Israel Sisterhood Cookbook* (Louisville, KY: Keneseth Israel Sisterhood, 1971), 125.

12. *My Old Kentucky Homes Cookbook* (St. Paul, MN: Cartwheel Publishing Company, n.d.), 17.

13. *Capital Eating in Kentucky* (Louisville, KY: American Cancer Society Kentucky Division, 1987), 74.

14. Margaret Fisk, ed., *The Cincinnati Cook Book* (Cincinnati: The Co-operative Society of the Children's Hospital, 1967), 129.

15. *Larue County Kitchens of Kentucky* (Hodgenville, KY: Hodgenville Women's Club, 1976), 125.

16. Barbara Wortham, *A Taste from Back Home* (Lakemont, GA: Copple House Books, Inc., 1983), 59.

17. Old Fashioned Day Committee, *Lebanon Junction's Old Fashion Cookbook* (Collierville, TN: Fundcraft Publishing, Inc., 1978), 15.

18. Hepburn Avenue Blockwatch, *Hepburn Avenue Cookbook* (Leawood, KS: Circulation Service, 1989), 43.

19. Patty Smyth, ed., *Cooking with Love and Memories, Irvine Chapter No. 357 O.E.S. Irvine, Kentucky* (Collierville, TN: Fundcraft Publishing, 1998), 29.

20. Berea Mennonite Church, *Heartwarming Recipes* (Olathe, KS: Cookbook Publishers, Inc., 1988), 42.

3. SIDES

1. *Kentucky Cookbook* (Phoenix, AZ: Golden West Publishers, 2000), 31.

2. Elizabeth Kremer, *Welcome Back to Pleasant Hill: More Recipes from the Trustees' House, Pleasant Hill, Kentucky* (Harrodsburg, KY: Pleasant Hill Press, 1977), 8, 11.

3. Eddie and Carolyn O'Daniel, *Recipes for History, Mystery & Southern Cooking: Springhill Plantation Bed and Breakfast & Winery* (Bloomfield, KY: Eddie O'Daniel, 2005), 59.

4. Cookbook Committee, *Kosair Cookbook* (Kansas City, MO: Circulation Service, 1968, 1973), 50–51.

5. Cherry Settle, Tommy Settle, and Edward G. Klemm Jr., *The Claudia Sanders Dinner House of Shelbyville, Kentucky, Cookbook* (Louisville, KY: Courier Graphics, 1979), 103.

6. *Center Cuisine: Recipes Collected by the Kentucky Center for the Arts Volunteers* (Louisville, KY: Kentucky Center for the Arts, 1995), 79.

7. *Cooking from the Heart* (Louisville, KY: Sacred Heart Academy, 1997), 56.

8. *Cook's Delight* (Shawnee Mission, KS: Circulation Service, 1968–1979), 80.

9. *A Walking Tour and Cooking Guide of Saint James Court* (Louisville, KY: The Saint James Court Association, 1976), 85–86.

10. *Favorite Recipes of Kentucky–Tennessee* (n.p.: Favorite Recipe Press, 1964), 91.

11. Mary Catherine Kirtley Young, *The Cherokee Triangle Olde Time Cookbook* (Louisville, KY: Cherokee Triangle Association, 1975), 59.

12. The Woman's Club of Central Kentucky, *The Best from the Blue Grass* (n.p.: The Woman's Club of Central Kentucky, 1968, 1974), 347.

13. Judy Fannin, ed., *Fannin Family and Friends Favorite Foods Often Fabulous! Always Fun!* (Waverly, IA: G & R Publishing Company, 2001), 208–9; Young, *Cherokee Triangle*, 30; Woman's Club of Central Kentucky, *Best from the Blue Grass*, 351–52.

14. Richard Hougen, *More Hougen Favorites* (Nashville, TN: The Parthenon Press, 1971), 82.

15. Chris Roseland, *The Best of Beaumont: A Recipe Collection* (Collierville, TN: Fundcraft Publishing, 1998), 44.

16. *"Owensboro's Very Famous" Moonlite Bar-B-Q Inn Inc.: Collection of Recipes* (Owensboro, KY: Moonlite Bar-B-Q Inn, 1986), 6; Patrick Bosley, ed., *Family Favorites from Moonlite: Recipes That Founded a Kentucky Tradition* (Owensboro, KY: Moonlite Bar-B-Q Inn, Inc., 2005), 45.

17. *Bicentennial Cookbook, 1789–1989, United Presbyterian Church, Lebanon, Kentucky: Favorite Recipes from Our Best Cooks* (Leawood, KS: Circulation Service, Inc., 1989), 43.

18. Cotta Circle, Lutheran Church Women, *Cookbook: Good Food Recipes, First Lutheran Church, Louisville, Kentucky* (Kansas City, MO: Circulation Service, 1966), 12.

19. The Laura Stewart Group of United Methodist Women St. Paul United Methodist Church, *Heavenly Creations, St. Paul United Methodist Church, Louisville, Kentucky* (Shawnee Mission, KS: Circulation Service, 1980), 35.

20. *Trigg County Cook Book: Six Hundred Favorite Family Recipes Gathered by the Members and Friends of the Trigg County Business & Pro-*

fessional Women's Club (Cadiz, KY: Trigg County Business & Professional Women's Club, n.d.), 150.

   21. *Berea's Best* (Berea, KY: Younger Women's Club, 1968), 193.

4. BREAD

   1. Sarah Fritschner, *Sarah Fritschner's Holidays: Menus and Recipes for the Fall Holiday Season* (Louisville: Butler Books, 2004), 32–33.

   2. Dorothea C. Cooper, ed., *Kentucky Hospitality: A 200-Year Tradition* (Louisville, KY: The Kentucky Federation of Women's Clubs, 1976, 1980, 1985), 113.

   3. *What's Bruin': Ballard High School Cook Book* (Kansas City, MO: Circulation Service, 1968), 46.

   4. Woman's Hospital Auxiliary, *Woodford Recipes* (Louisville, KY: Grimes Press, 1959, 1961, 1967), 17.

   5. Madonna Smith Echols, *The Crowning Recipes of Kentucky* (Louisville, KY: Marathon International Publishing Company, 1986), 43.

   6. Sam Carson and A. W. Vick, *Hillbilly Cookin 2* (Sevierville, TN: C & F Sales, Inc., 1972), 12.

   7. Ronni Lundy, *Shuck Beans, Stack Cakes, and Honest Fried Chicken: The Heart and Soul of Southern Country Kitchens* (New York: The Atlantic Monthly Press, 1991), 277.

   8. *BGMU Cookbook 2007* (Bowling Green, KY: Bowling Green Municipal Utilities, 2007), 13.

   9. Betty Jane Donahoe, *How to Boil Water* (Ashtabula, OH: River City Publishers, 1972), 22, 141.

   10. *Tanker's Range* (Ft. Knox, KY: Officers' Wives Club, 1963), 236–37.

   11. Susanna Thomas, *Thelma's Treasures: The Secret Recipes of "The Best Cook in Harrodsburg"* (Harrodsburg, KY: Little Barter Press, 1992), 52.

   12. Bobbie Smith Bryant, *Passions of the Black Patch: Cooking and Quilting in Western Kentucky* (Louisville, KY: Butler Books, 2012), 87.

   13. *Derby Entertaining: Traditional Kentucky Recipes* (Kuttawa, KY: McClanahan Publishing House, 2008), 11.

   14. Fidelis Class, *Bethel Cookbook* (Kansas City, MO: North American Press, 1954), 46–47; Mary Elizabeth Dedman and Thomas Curry Dedman Jr., *Beaumont Inn Special Recipes* (Harrodsburg, KY: Beaumont Inn, 1983), 69.

15. Richard T. Hougen, *Look No Further: A Cookbook of Favorite Recipes from Boone Tavern Hotel, Berea College, Kentucky* (New York: Abingdon Press, 1951, 1953, 1955), 3.

16. *Cooking with Middletown Woman's Club* (Middletown, KY: Middletown Woman's Club, 1980), 17.

17. *Louisville Collegiate School, 75th Anniversary Cookbook* (Olathe, KS: Cookbook Publishers, Inc., 1991), 121.

18. *Cooking through the Years with Bullitt County Homemakers* (Collierville, TN: Fundcraft Publishing, 1984), 75.

19. *Kitchens of Barren County Homemakers* (Barren County, KY: Barren County Progress, 1980), 31; *Hot Browne: A Second Helping* (Lenexa, KS: Cookbook Publishers, 2003), 178; Judy Fannin, ed., *Fannin Family and Friends Favorite Foods Often Fabulous! Always Fun!* (Waverly, IA: G & R Publishing Company, 2001), 236.

20. Linda G. Hatcher, *Southern Bread Winners* (n.p.: Dot Gibson Publications, 1992).

5. Bourbon

1. *Cooking with Bourbon* (Louisville, KY: Recipe Unlimited, n.d.), 90–91.

2. W. C. Whitfield, ed., *Here's How* (Asheville, NC: Three Mountaineers, Inc., 1941), 13; Irvin S. Cobb, *Irvin S. Cobb's Own Recipe Book* (Louisville, KY: Frankfort Distilleries, 1936), 44.

3. Richard B. Harwell, *The Mint Julep* (Charlottesville: University Press of Virginia, 1975), 1, 38, 43; Whitfield, *Here's How*, 23; Jody Johnson, ed., *Poll-ette Hostess: Family Favorites* (Bowling Green, KY: National Council of Poll-ettes, 1967, 1970, 1974, 1977), 59; Greta Hipp Burkhart, *Kentucky Always in Season* (Kuttawa, KY: McClanahan Publishing Company, 2001), 24; Soule Smith, *The Mint Julep, the Very Dream of Drinks* (Lexington, KY: The Gravesend Press, 1949, 1964), 3; Joe Nickell, *The Kentucky Mint Julep* (Lexington: University Press of Kentucky, 2003), 16, 27; Cobb, *Cobb's Own Recipe Book*, 45.

4. Colonel Michael Edward Masters, *Hospitality: Kentucky Style* (Bardstown, KY: Equine Writer's Press, 2003), 238.

5. *Somethin's Cookin at LG&E* (Louisville, KY: LG&E Employees Association, Inc., 1986), 15.

6. *A. Lincoln Legacy Tasting Tour* (Springfield, KY: City of Springfield, 2008), 66.

7. Tom Hoge, *The Bourbon Cookbook* (Harrisburg, PA: Stackpole Books, 1975), 279.

8. C. F. Lawlor, *The Mixicologist* (Cincinnati: Lawlor & Co., 1895), 98.

9. Lawlor, *The Mixicologist*, 49, 50, 55.

10. Whitfield, *Here's How*, 15.

11. Dana Fendley, ed., *Kentucky Kitchens, Volume II: I Hear You Calling Me* (Nashville: Favorite Recipes Press, 1989), 70.

12. Bernie Lubbers, *Bourbon Whiskey Our Native Spirit: Sour Mash and Sweet Adventures* (Indianapolis: Blue River Press, 2011), 172.

13. Joy Perrine and Susan Reigler, *The Kentucky Bourbon Cocktail Book* (Lexington: The University Press of Kentucky, 2009), 34–35.

14. The Junior League of Louisville, Inc., *CordonBluegrass: Blue Ribbon Recipes from Kentucky* (Memphis: Wimmer Brothers, 1988), 30.

15. The Junior League of Louisville, *The Cooking Book* (Louisville, KY: The Junior League of Louisville, 1978), 31.

16. *Festive Firsts* (Louisville, KY: Children's Hospital Auxiliary, 1976), 190; Barbara Seiber, ed., *Bellarmine Designers' Show House Cookbook* (Louisville, KY: The Bellarmine Women's Council, 1996), 26; *The Cincinnati Cook Book* (Cincinnati: The Co-operative Society of the Children's Hospital, 1967), 279; Teresa Simpson, *In the Kitchen with Ann* (Kearney, NE: Morris Press Cookbooks, 2013), 7.

17. Marcia Hasenour Larkin, *Hasenour's: The History of a Louisville Restaurant Tradition* (Louisville, KY: Hasenour Press, 2001), 82.

18. Barbara Cox, ed., *Love Is . . . #2 in Your Collection of "Breckinridge Co. Homemakers" Recipes* (Breckinridge County, KY: Breckinridge County Homemakers, 1982), 137.

19. Kelli Oakley and Jayna Oakley, *Kentucky TALEgating II: More Stories with Sauce* (Morley, MO: Acclaim Press, 2007), 169.

6. Desserts

1. Shirley Corriher, *CookWise: The Hows & Whys of Successful Cooking with over 230 Great-Tasting Recipes* (New York: William Morrow & Company, Inc., 1997), 102–3.

2. Maggie Green, *The Kentucky Fresh Cookbook* (Lexington: The University Press of Kentucky, 2011), 90.

3. *The Farmington Cookbook* (Louisville, KY: Farmington, 1979), 330; *Favorite Fare II* (Louisville, KY: The Woman's Club of Louisville, 1984), 28; Sharon Thompson, *Flavors of Kentucky* (Kuttawa, KY: Mc-Clanahan Publishing House, 2006), 137; *A Slice of Kentucky: Sharing Our Recipes* (Kuttawa, KY: McClanahan Publishing House, 2003), 165; Jody Johnson, ed., *Poll-ette Hostess: Family Favorites* (Bowling Green, KY: National Council of Poll-ettes, 1967, 1970, 1974, 1977), 41.

4. Johnson, *Poll-ette Hostess*, 41.

5. Paula Cunningham, ed., *Sample West Kentucky: A Restaurant Guide with Menus and Recipes* (Kuttawa, KY: McClanahan Publishing House, 1985), 47; Patti's Enterprises, *Miss Patti's Cook Book* (Kuttawa, KY: McClanahan Publishing House, 1997), 169.

6. Linda Allison-Lewis, *Kentucky's Best: Fifty Years of Great Recipes* (Lexington: University Press of Kentucky, 1998), 222; Marty Godbey, *Dining in Historic Kentucky* (Kuttawa, KY: McClanahan Publishing House, 1992), 107; Donna Gill, Ellen Gill, and Terry Gill, *What I Like Best About Dining with the Gills. . . .*, 4th ed. (Shelbyville, KY: Science Hill Inn, 1990), 35.

7. *Cooking Through the Years with Bullitt County Homemakers* (Collierville, TN: Fundcraft Publishing, Inc., 1984), 62; *From the Kitchens of Barren County Homemakers* (Barren County, KY: Barren County Progress, 1980), 154; *Still Cookin' after All These Years: The Presidents Club of South-Central Kentucky* (Bowling Green, KY, 1990), 125; *Cooking with Middletown Women's Club* (Waverley, IA: G and R Publishing Company, 1980), 81; *Cookin' from Scratch: Taylor County Homemakers* (Collierville, TN: Fundcraft Publishing, 1984), 69.

8. Greta Hipp Burkhart, *Kentucky Always in Season* (Kuttawa, KY: McClanahan Publishing Company, 2001), 125.

9. *A Slice of Kentucky: Sharing Our Recipes* (Kuttawa, KY: McClanahan Publishing House, 2003), 166; Joseph E. Dabney, *Smokehouse Ham, Spoon Bread & Scuppernong Wine: The Folklore and Art of Southern Appalachian Cooking* (Nashville: Cumberland House, 1998), 411.

10. *Favorite Fare II*, 8, 9, 11, 26.

11. *Favorite Fare* (Louisville, KY: The Woman's Club of Louisville, 1968, 1972, 1976), 199.

12. Charles Patteson with Craig Emerson, *Charles Patteson's Kentucky Cooking* (New York: Harper & Row Publishers, 1988), 139; *The Farmington Cookbook* (Louisville, KY: Farmington, 1979), 321.

13. Minnie C. Fox, *The Blue Grass Cookbook* (Lexington: University Press of Kentucky, 1904, 2005), 213.

14. Elizabeth Kremer, *We Make You Kindly Welcome* (Harrodsburg, KY: Pleasant Hill Press, 1970), 67, 70; Allison-Lewis, *Kentucky's Best*, 236.

15. *Partytime in Kentucky* (Memphis: Wimmer Brothers Books, 1982), 122.

16. *Prescriptions for Cooks, Volume II* (Louisville, KY: Woman's Auxiliary to the Jefferson County Medical Society, 1971), 129.

17. *Cook's Delight* (Louisville, KY: Plainview Pre-School, Inc., 1979), 7.

18. *Bluegrass Winners: A Cookbook* (Lexington, KY: The Garden Club of Lexington, 1985), 287.

19. *Derbytown Winners Cookbook* (Louisville, KY: Crescent Hill Woman's Club, 1971), 221.

20. *Burkesville, Kentucky, Now and Then, A Bicentennial Celebration: 200 Years of Treasured Recipes* (Burkesville, KY, 2010), 129.

21. Jane Lee Rankin, *Cookin' Up a Storm: The Life and Recipes of Annie Johnson* (South Fallsburg, NY: Grace Publishers, 1998), 146.

22. Maggie Green, *The Kentucky Fresh Cookbook* (Lexington: University Press of Kentucky, 2011), 89; Kremer, *We Make You Kindly Welcome*, 18.

Bibliography

A. Lincoln Legacy Tasting Tour. Springfield, KY: The City of Springfield, 2008.

Allison-Lewis, Linda. *Kentucky's Best: Fifty Years of Great Recipes.* Lexington: University Press of Kentucky, 1998.

Anderson, Janet Alm. *A Taste of Kentucky.* Lexington: The University Press of Kentucky, 1986.

Anderson, Jean. "Kentucky Burgoo." epicurious.com.

Barkley, Alben W. *That Reminds Me.* Garden City, NY: Doubleday & Company, Inc., 1954.

Beard, Daniel. *Camp-Lore and Woodcraft.* Mineola, NY: Dover Publications, 2006.

Berea Mennonite Church. *Heartwarming Recipes.* Olathe, KS: Cookbook Publishers, 1988.

Berea's Best. Berea, KY: Younger Women's Club, 1968.

Berry, Wes. *The Kentucky Barbecue Book.* Lexington: University Press of Kentucky, 2013.

BGMU Cookbook 2007. Bowling Green, KY: Bowling Green Municipal Utilities, 2007.

Bicentennial Cookbook, 1789–1989, United Presbyterian Church, Lebanon, Kentucky: Favorite Recipes from Our Best Cooks. Leawood, KS: Circulation Service, Inc. 1989.

Bluegrass Winners: A Cookbook. Lexington, KY: The Garden Club of Lexington, 1985.

Bosley, Patrick, ed. *Family Favorites from Moonlite: Recipes That Founded a Kentucky Tradition.* Owensboro, KY: Moonlite Bar-B-Q Inn, Inc., 2005.

Bridwell, Margaret M. *Kentucky Fare: A Recipe Book of Some of Kentucky's Mouth Watering Specialties.* n.p.: Margaret M. Bridwell, 1953.

Bryant, Bobbie Smith. *Passions of the Black Patch: Cooking and Quilting in Western Kentucky.* Louisville, KY: Butler Books, 2012.

Burkesville, Kentucky, Now and Then, A Bicentennial Celebration: 200 Years of Treasured Recipes. Burkesville, KY, 2010.

Burkhart, Greta Hipp. *Kentucky Always in Season.* Kuttawa, KY: McClanahan Publishing Company, 2001.

Cabbage Patch Circle. *Cabbage Patch: Famous Kentucky Recipes.* Louisville, KY: Gateway Press, Inc., 1952, 1954, 1956.

Capital Eating in Kentucky. Louisville, KY: American Cancer Society Kentucky Division, 1987.

Carson, Sam, and A. W. Vick. *Hillbilly Cookin 2.* Sevierville, TN: C & F Sales, Inc., 1972.

Center Cuisine: Recipes Collected by the Kentucky Center for the Arts Volunteers. Louisville, KY: Kentucky Center for the Arts, 1995.

Cobb, Irvin S. *Irvin S. Cobb's Own Recipe Book.* Louisville, KY: Frankfort Distilleries, 1936.

Cookbook Committee. *Kosair Cookbook.* Kansas City, MO: Circulation Service, 1968, 1973.

Cook Book 1982: United Methodist Women. Lexington, KY: First United Methodist Church, 1982.

Cookin' from Scratch: Taylor County Homemakers. Collierville, TN: Fundcraft Publishing, 1984.

Cooking from the Heart. Louisville, KY: Sacred Heart Academy, 1997.

Cooking through the Years with Bullitt County Homemakers. Collierville, TN: Fundcraft Publishing Inc., 1984.

Cooking with Bourbon. Louisville, KY: Recipes Unlimited, n.d.

Cooking with Middletown Woman's Club. Middletown, KY: Middletown Woman's Club, 1980.

Cook's Delight. Louisville, KY: Plainview Pre-School, Inc., 1979.

Cook's Delight. Shawnee Mission, KS: Circulation Service, 1968–1979.

Cooper, Dorothea C., ed. *Kentucky Hospitality: A 200-Year Tradition.* Louisville, KY: The Kentucky Federation of Women's Clubs, 1976, 1980, 1985.

Corriher, Shirley. *CookWise: The Hows & Whys of Successful Cooking with over 230 Great-Tasting Recipes.* New York: William Morrow & Company, Inc., 1997.

Cotta Circle, Lutheran Church Women. *Cookbook: Good Food Recipes, First Lutheran Church, Louisville, Kentucky.* Kansas City, MO: Circulation Service, 1966.

Cox, Barbara, ed. *Love Is . . . #2 in Your Collection of "Breckinridge Co. Homemakers" Recipes.* Breckinridge County, KY: Breckinridge County Homemakers, 1982.

Craig, Berry. *True Tales of Old-Time Kentucky Politics: Bombast, Bourbon, and Burgoo.* Charleston, SC: The History Press, 2009.

Cunningham, Paula, ed. *Sample West Kentucky: A Restaurant Guide with Menus and Recipes.* Kuttawa, KY: McClanahan Publishing House, 1985.

Dabney, Joseph E. *Smokehouse Ham, Spoon Bread & Scuppernong Wine: The Folklore and Art of Southern Appalachian Cooking.* Nashville: Cumberland House, 1998.

Dedman, Mary Elizabeth, and Thomas Curry Dedman Jr. *Beaumont Inn Special Recipes.* Harrodsburg, KY: Beaumont Inn, 1983.

Derby Entertaining: Traditional Kentucky Recipes. Kuttawa, KY: McClanahan Publishing House, 2008.

Derbytown Winners Cookbook. Louisville, KY: Crescent Hill Woman's Club, 1971.

Donahoe, Betty Jane. *How to Boil Water.* Ashtabula, OH: River City Publishers, 1972.

Echols, Madonna Smith. *The Crowning Recipes of Kentucky.* Louisville, KY: Marathon International Publishing Company, 1986.

Fannin, Judy, ed. *Fannin Family and Friends Favorite Foods Often Fabulous! Always Fun!* Waverly, IA: G & R Publishing Company, 2001.

The Farmington Cookbook. Louisville, KY: Farmington, 1979.

Favorite Fare. Louisville, KY: The Woman's Club of Louisville, 1968.

Favorite Fare II. Louisville, KY: The Woman's Club of Louisville, 1984.

Favorite Recipes of Kentucky-Tennessee. n.p.: Favorite Recipe Press, 1964.

Fendley, Dana, ed. *Kentucky Kitchens, Volume II: I Hear You Calling Me.* Nashville: Favorite Recipes Press, 1989.

Fidelis Class. *Bethel Cookbook.* Kansas City, MO: North American Press, 1954.

Finley, John, ed. *The Courier-Journal Kentucky Cookbook.* Louisville, KY: The Courier-Journal and Louisville Times Company, 1985.

Fisk, Margaret, ed. *The Cincinnati Cook Book.* Cincinnati: The Co-operative Society of the Children's Hospital, 1967.

Flexner, Marion. *Out of Kentucky Kitchens.* New York: Bramhall House, 1949.

Fox, Minnie C. *The Blue Grass Cookbook.* Lexington: University Press of Kentucky, 1904, 2005.

Fritschner, Sarah. *Sarah Fritschner's Holidays: Menus and Recipes for the Fall Holiday Season.* Louisville, KY: Butler Books, 2004.

From the Kitchens of Barren County Homemakers. Barren County, KY: Barren County Progress, 1980.

Gill, Donna, Ellen Gill, and Terry Gill. *What I Like Best about Dinning with the Gills*. 4th edition. Shelbyville, KY: Science Hill Inn, 1990.

Godbey, Marty. *Dining in Historic Kentucky*. Kuttawa, KY: McClanahan Publishing House, 1992.

Green, Maggie. *The Kentucky Fresh Cookbook*. Lexington: University Press of Kentucky, 2011.

Harper-Bach, Barbara. *The Derby Party Cooking Clinic*. n.p.: Barbara Harper-Bach, 2013.

Harwell, Richard B. *The Mint Julep*. Charlottesville: University Press of Virginia, 1975.

Hawkins, Nancy and Arthur. *The American Regional Cookbook: Recipes from Yesterday and Today for the Modern Cook*. Englewood Cliffs, NJ: Prentice-Hall, Inc., 1976.

Hepburn Avenue Blockwatch. *Hepburn Avenue Cookbook*. Leawood, KS: Circulation Service, 1989.

Hoge, Tom. *The Bourbon Cookbook*. Harrisburg, PA: Stackpole Books, 1975.

Hot Browne. Louisville, KY: Harvey Browne Memorial Presbyterian Church, 1984.

Hot Browne: A Second Helping. Lenexa, KS: Cookbook Publishers, 2003.

Hougen, Richard T. *Look No Further: A Cookbook of Favorite Recipes from Boone Tavern Hotel, Berea College, Kentucky*. New York: Abingdon Press, 1951, 1953, 1955.

———. *More Hougen Favorites*. Nashville: The Parthenon Press, 1971.

Johnson, Jody, ed. *Poll-ette Hostess: Family Favorites*. Bowling Green, KY: National Council of Poll-ettes, 1967, 1970, 1974, 1977.

Joyce, Justin, and Stephan MacIntyre. *Burgoo: Food for Comfort*. Vancouver, BC: Figure 1 Publishing, 2013.

The Junior League of Louisville. *The Cooking Book*. Louisville, KY: The Junior League of Louisville, 1978.

———. *CordonBluegrass: Blue Ribbon Recipes from Kentucky*. Memphis: Wimmer Brothers, 1988.

Keneseth Israel Sisterhood. *Keneseth Israel Sisterhood Cookbook*. Louisville, KY: Keneseth Israel Sisterhood, 1971.

Kentucky Cookbook. Phoenix, AZ: Golden West Publishers, 2000.

Kentucky Heritage Recipes. Louisville, KY: Historic Homes Foundation, 1976, 1977, 1978, 1980.

Kentucky's Winning Recipes. Shawnee Mission, KS: Circulation Service, 1984.

Kremer, Elizabeth. *Welcome Back to Pleasant Hill: More Recipes from the Trustees' House, Pleasant Hill, Kentucky.* Harrodsburg, KY: Pleasant Hill Press, 1977.

———. *We Make You Kindly Welcome.* Harrodsburg, KY: Pleasant Hill Press, 1970.

Larkin, Marcia Hasenour. *Hasenour's: The History of a Louisville Restaurant Tradition.* Louisville, KY: Hasenour Press, 2001.

Larue County Kitchens of Kentucky. Hodgenville, KY: Hodgenville Women's Club, 1976.

Laura Stewart Group of United Methodist Women St. Paul United Methodist Church, The. *Heavenly Creations, St. Paul United Methodist Church, Louisville, Kentucky.* Shawnee Mission, KS: Circulation Service, 1980.

Lawlor, C. F. *The Mixicologist.* Cincinnati: Lawlor & Co., 1895.

Louisville Collegiate School, 75th Anniversary Cookbook. Olathe, KS: Cookbook Publishers, Inc., 1991.

Lubbers, Bernie. *Bourbon Whiskey Our Native Spirit: Sour Mash and Sweet Adventures.* Indianapolis: Blue River Press, 2011.

Lundy, Jonathan. *Jonathan's Bluegrass Table: Redefining Kentucky Cuisine.* Louisville, KY: Butler Books, 2009.

Lundy, Ronni. *Shuck Beans, Stack Cakes, and Honest Fried Chicken: The Heart and Soul of Southern Country Kitchens.* New York: The Atlantic Monthly Press, 1991.

Lustig, Lillie S., S. Claire Sondheim, and Sarah Rensel. *The Southern Cook Book of Fine Old Recipes.* Reading, PA: Culinary Arts Press, 1935.

Marinades and Rubs: 40 Tantalizing Recipes to Stimulate Your Palette and Add Sparkle to Your Meals! Bath, UK: Paragon Books, Ltd., 2007.

Marshall, Lillian. *The Courier-Journal & Times Cook Book.* Louisville, KY: The Louisville Courier-Journal & Louisville Times Company, 1971.

Masters, Colonel Michael Edward. *Hospitality: Kentucky Style.* Bardstown, KY: Equine Writer's Press, 2003.

Maxwell, Jeff. *Secrets of the M*A*S*H Mess: The Lost Recipes of Private Igor.* Nashville: Cumberland House, 1997.

The Monterey Cookbook. Monterey, KY: Cedar Creek Community School, 1986.

Moss, Robert F. *Barbecue: The History of an American Institution.* Tuscaloosa: The University of Alabama Press, 2010.

My Old Kentucky Homes Cookbook. St. Paul, MN: Cartwheel Publishing Company, n.d.

Nemec, David. *The Beer and Whiskey League: The Illustrated History of the American Association—Baseball's Renegade League.* Guilford, CT: The Lyon Press, 2004.

Newton, Jacky. *Franklinton Friends and Families.* Collierville, TN: Fundcraft Publishing, 2005.

Nickell, Joe. *The Kentucky Mint Julep.* Lexington: University Press of Kentucky, 2003.

Oakley, Kelli, and Jayna Oakley. *Kentucky TALEgating II: More Stories with Sauce.* Morley, MO: Acclaim Press, 2007.

O'Daniel, Eddie and Carolyn. *Recipes for History, Mystery & Southern Cooking: Springhill Plantation Bed and Breakfast & Winery.* Bloomfield, KY: Eddie O'Daniel, 2005.

Old Fashioned Day Committee. *Lebanon Junction's Old Fashion Cookbook.* Collierville, TN: Fundcraft Publishing, Inc., 1978.

"Owensboro's Very Famous" Moonlite Bar-B-Q Inn Inc.: Collection of Recipes. Owensboro, KY: Moonlite Bar-B-Q Inn, 1986.

Partytime in Kentucky. Memphis: Wimmer Brothers Book, 1982.

Patteson, Charles, with Craig Emerson. *Charles Patteson's Kentucky Cooking.* New York: Harper & Row Publishers, 1988.

Patti's Enterprises. *Miss Patti's Cook Book.* Kuttawa, KY: McClanahan Publishing House, 1997.

Perrine, Joy, and Susan Reigler. *The Kentucky Bourbon Cocktail Book.* Lexington: The University Press of Kentucky, 2009.

Philpot, Mrs. Lawrence (Lou Ann), ed. *Murray Woman's Club Cookbook.* 7th edition. Nashville: Reed Publishing Company, 1972.

Prescriptions for Cooks, Volume II. Louisville, KY: Woman's Auxiliary to the Jefferson County Medical Society, 1971.

The Queen's Daughters, Inc. *Entertaining the Louisville Way.* Louisville, KY: The Queen's Daughters, 1969.

Ramage, James A., and Andrea S. Watkins. *Kentucky Rising: Democracy, Slavery, and Culture from the Early Republic to the Civil War.* Lexington: University Press of Kentucky, 2011.

Ranck, George Washington. *The History of Lexington, Kentucky.* Cincinnati: Robert Clarke & Co., 1872.

Rankin, Jane Lee. *Cookin' Up a Storm: The Life and Recipes of Annie John-son*. South Fallsburg, NY: Grace Publishers, 1998.

Roseland, Chris. *The Best of Beaumont*. Collierville, TN: Fundcraft Publishing, 1998.

Scaggs, Deirdre A., and Andrew W. McGraw. *The Historic Kentucky Kitchen: Traditional Recipes for Today's Cook*. Lexington: University Press of Kentucky, 2013.

Settle, Cherry, Tommy Settle, and Edward G. Klemm Jr. *The Claudia Sanders Dinner House of Shelbyville, Kentucky, Cookbook*. Louisville, KY: Courier Graphics, 1979.

Simpson, Teresa. *In the Kitchen with Ann*. Kearney, NE: Morris Press Cookbooks, 2013.

A Slice of Kentucky: Sharing Our Recipes. Kuttawa, KY: McClanahan Publishing House, 2003.

Smith, Soule. *The Mint Julep, the Very Dream of Drinks*. Lexington, KY: The Gravesend Press, 1949, 1964.

Smyth, Patty, ed. *Cooking with Love and Memories, Irvine Chapter No. 357 O.E.S. Irvine, Kentucky*. Collierville, TN: Fundcraft Publishing, 1998.

Somethin's Cooking at LG&E. Louisville, KY: LG&E Employees Association, Inc., 1986.

Staff. *Brighton, Illinois, Centennial Cookbook, Famous for Burgoo Soup, 1869–1969*. Souvenir edition. Brighton, IL, 1969.

Still Cookin after All These Years: The Presidents Club of South-Central Kentucky. Bowling Green, KY, 1990.

Tanker's Range. Ft. Knox, KY: Officers' Wives Club, 1963.

Thomas, Susanna. *Thelma's Treasures: The Secret Recipes of "The Best Cook in Harrodsburg."* Harrodsburg, KY: Little Barter Press, 1992.

Thompson, Sharon. *Flavors of Kentucky*. Kuttawa, KY: McClanahan Publishing House, 2006.

To Market, To Market. Owensboro, KY: The Junior League of Owensboro, Inc., 1993.

Trigg County Cook Book: Six Hundred Favorite Family Recipes Gathered by the Members and Friends of the Trigg County Business & Professional Women's Club. Cadiz, KY: Trigg County Business & Professional Women's Club, n.d.

Villas, James. *Stews, Bogs & Burgoos: Recipes from the Great American Stewpot*. New York: William Morrow and Company, Inc., 1997.

BIBLIOGRAPHY

A Walking Tour and Cooking Guide of Saint James Court. Louisville, KY: The Saint James Court Association, 1976.

Wallace, Gene. *The ABC's of Illinois Festivals: Apples, Burgoo & Cornbread.* Urbana: University of Illinois, 1959.

What's Bruin': Ballard High School Cook Book. Kansas City, MO: Circulation Service, 1968.

Whitfield, W. C., ed. *Here's How.* Asheville, NC: Three Mountaineers, Inc., 1941.

Woman's Club of Central Kentucky, The. *The Best from the Blue Grass.* n.p.: The Woman's Club of Central Kentucky, 1968, 1974.

Woman's Hospital Auxiliary. *Woodford Recipes.* Louisville, KY: Grimes Press, 1959, 1961, 1967.

Wortham, Barbara. *A Taste from Back Home.* Lakemont, GA: Copple House Books, Inc., 1983.

Young, Mary Catherine Kirtley. *The Cherokee Triangle Olde Time Cookbook.* Louisville, KY: Cherokee Triangle Association, 1975.

Index